OVERCOMING ANXIETY & PANIC ATTACKS

TWO BOOKS TO HELP YOU REGAIN CONTROL OF YOUR LIFE

ED JONES

BOOK 1:

Overcoming Anxiety - *How Anxiety is killing you and what to do About It*

INTRODUCTION

Anxiety can kill you. It sounds a bit strong, but it's true. Here, I mean it in the metaphorical sense as anxiety and stress can stop you from living your full potential. I also mean it in the very literal sense.

I think that's a huge waste.

Everyone goes through times in their lives when they're stressed or anxious. Some people can grab stress by the horns and power through whatever is happening. Others (myself included) have a harder time of navigating the increases in tension and apprehension.

Anxiety is a mental health issue at its core, but when prolonged it can lead to very real and very debilitating symptoms as well as disorders. These can start as fairly innocuous things (like digestive problems or unexplained skin conditions). When left unchecked, issues can get worse and lead to disorders like depression and insomnia.

After an extended period of constant anxiety and stress, your body is much more prone to serious, sometimes life-threatening conditions like heart disease, hypertension and diabetes. Some people are starting to attribute this constant stress on the body to certain types of cancer, too.

With all these negative outcomes, why would anyone want to spend their life like this: depressed, anxious or afraid? It's not fair. I want to help.

Having experienced a whole heap of problems with stress, anxiety and depression, I can honestly relate when people tell me they're having a hard time.

Anxiety was killing my social life because I was suffering with agoraphobia, meaning I was too frightened to leave the house. Anxiety was also directly impacting my finances — I couldn't leave the house so I couldn't go to work; I lost my job (compounding my misery)! When I recognized that my anxiety was starting to take hold of me physically, I knew I had to do something. My back was constantly knotted and I could barely move my neck. I was constantly exhausted. I would have panic attacks almost every time I left the house and my stomach was constantly bloated and uncomfortable, no matter what I ate. I knew I had to make a change and fix myself before this horrible condition got the better of me!

Thankfully, there is a wealth of information out there that's easily accessible. Not all of it is great and not all of it worked for me, but some of it did. Some of it made a small bit of a difference and some of it made ALL the difference. Thanks to everything I've learned, I'm now living my life to the fullest! I have a great job that I love, I have a beautiful woman by my side and I've got more energy than I ever knew was possible!

And the great news is that you can do it, too!

There are a number of ways to combat anxiety and stress. I've found that some of the most powerful and easy ways are all natural solutions.

I know, I know; it sounds a bit like a hippy wrote that, but I promise you, the strategies in this book can change your life. They've changed mine. I'm no longer worried about having panic attacks. I no longer have agoraphobia. I'm no longer a hypochondriac. I got rid of my fear of heights and I'm more confident than I've ever been.

And all that took only three weeks of working through the steps I've shared with you in this book.

You're probably skeptical. But know that I didn't have a clue what I was doing at first, either. With a guide like this, you'll be able to pull it off much faster!

I wrote this book for a range of people with a variety of challenges. As such, I cover a lot of ground. There's going to be some really relevant stuff in here to help you, and perhaps some not-so-relevant stuff, too.

This book has been written so you can quickly access the tools that are most pertinent to you. That means you don't need to read the book cover to cover. In fact, I expect most people wouldn't!

The only thing I really recommend is that <u>everyone should read **THE KEY TECHNIQUE**</u> as this will give the quickest (and sometimes, the most potent) return for your time.

If that hasn't resolved your issue completely, jump straight into the chapter(s) most relevant to you. Think of it like a buffet: you pick and choose the things of interest to you.

Don't feel guilty if you don't read the whole book. Take value out of the parts I wrote just for you and get the tools to improve your life!

What Type of Issues Will This Book Help Me Overcome?

In my previous book, *Beating Panic Attacks*, I ran through some of the steps that I took in order to resolve my own issues with panic attacks. I touched on a few potential techniques to use and I really wanted to expand them further as they apply to more than those suffering from panic.

This book focuses on the associated struggles around anxiety in general. I'll be covering everything from affirmations to supplements. Theses tools can be incredibly powerful in helping in a range of challenges that people face: depression, General Anxiety Order (GAD), phobias, insomnia and many more.

Even if you don't have a diagnosis of any of these but you know you feel stressed, the tips and exercises in this book can really help.

I'll address the key challenges in detail in their individual chapters, but just know that these techniques and tools really can help anyone to live a more empowered and stress-free life!

BREATHING

*W*hy Is Controlling Your Breath Important?

Everyone's gotta breathe, right? If you don't breathe, you don't do a whole lot of anything else. But what's so important about managing your breathing? Perhaps you're thinking, *"I've gotten this far in my life and I've managed to breath just fine on my own!"*

Quite right. And for many people, learning how to *"breathe"* is not something that interests them.

However, they should be **VERY** interested in it.

In our case, we're talking about how breathing can alleviate symptoms of anxiety and related conditions — it does it almost miraculously.

Anxious Breathing

When we feel anxious, our breathing changes. We start to

take short, quick, shallow breaths, sometimes even hyper-ventilating. It's commonly referred to as *"over-breathing."*

This book is going to provide techniques for managing *"over-breathing."* This type of breathing can actually make you feel even more anxious by increasing your heart rate, causing dizziness and headaches (not the things you want when you're trying to calm down).

It's amazing how real the physical symptoms can be when we're talking about just thoughts in your head and a bit of breathing. The upshot is that you can fix both of these issues with the same tools.

Breathing techniques are fantastic, portable tools that you can use whenever you're feeling anxious. However, some of them do require some practice (not a lot, though, don't worry).

The reason they work so well is because it quickly and effec-tively turns off your body's fight-or-flight response, which is almost entirely the reason you experience the physical symp-toms relating to anxiety.

Panic attacks and GAD are examples of where your body is in fight-or-flight mode for either a short or a sustained period of time. With other conditions (like depression), it could be the result of the body having been in fight-or-flight mode for so long that it starts to withdraw, and generates negative thoughts associated with all the energy consumed with fighting for such a long time.

Because breathing got us in to this, it can damn sure get us out of it.

Stick with me as you're about to learn something that can change your life...

Key Technique

There is a lot of information in the book. Hopefully, at least some of it, helpful.

If you're anything like me, you'll buy a self-help book, read through it, take notes maybe and get motivated. Then you'll probably only remember one thing from the book.

Well I'll save you some time — *this is that ONE thing: the 4-7-8 breath.*

All of the techniques outlined in this book will help someone. Some of them are specifically for experiences that occur in the moment, like panic attacks. Some are for ongoing issues such as depression or GAD. But all of them are designed to help you take control of your physiology again.

What is the 4-7-8 breath?

Developed by Dr. Andrew Weil, the 4-7-8 breath has been described as *"a natural tranquilizer for the nervous system."* This sounds like just the thing we need!

This method has some of the same de-stressing benefits as

mediation and helps to relax your body almost instantly. A few quotes from its inventor help explain the technique:

"Practicing regular, mindful breathing can be calming and energizing and can even help with stress-related health problems ranging from panic attacks to digestive disorders."

"Since breathing is something we can control and regulate, it is a useful tool for achieving a relaxed and clear state of mind."

"[Breathing is] the single best anti-anxiety method I've found."

Why use it?

The reason I highlight this technique is because it's simple and it's easy to remember when you're in a panicked state. It also works really, really well.

This was the first breathing technique I learned and it played a **HUGE** part in my journey to alleviate my anxiety and panic attacks.

You can do it in public without looking like a crazy person (important if you're having a panic attack in a public place and you can't take yourself off to one side).

In this modern world, we can be constantly bombarded with things that leave us feeling both insecure and stressed. This routine can lead our bodies and minds to become accustomed to living in a constant state of fight-or-flight, which can cause all sorts of problems in the body, like

- Elevated stress hormones.

- Shallow breathing.
- Prompting panic and anxiety attacks.
- Raising blood pressure.

These are all natural and normal reactions from our stress response system, but are made worse by our environments. Fortunately, using techniques like the 4-7-8 breath, you can get control of your physiology again both quickly and easily.

Method

So, how do you practice this magical technique?

1. Sit comfortably in a straight-back position.
2. Place the tip of your tongue on the ridge of your gums, just behind your front teeth.
3. Expand your diaphragm and slowly inhale through your nose for a count of **four.**
4. Hold your breath for another count of **seven.**
5. Open your mouth slightly and exhale for **eight** counts, contracting your diaphragm.
6. Repeat this cycle four times.

You always want to inhale quietly through your nose and exhale audibly through your mouth. The tip of your tongue stays in the same position the whole time. Exhalation should take twice as long as inhalation.

The total time you spend on each round is not important; the ratio of 4:7:8 is what counts (pun intended). If you are struggling to hold your breath, speed the exercise up to suit, but keep to the ratio of 4:7:8 for the last three cycles. After some practice, you'll be able to slow it down as you get used to inhaling and exhaling more deeply.

The whole process only takes a couple of minutes and can instantly turn off your fight-or-flight response. It's perfect if you're having a panic attack or just need to relax quickly.

Dr. Weil recommends practicing the 'relaxing breath' twice a day for at least six to eight weeks to perfect it.

Once you've got the hang of it, Dr. Weil has also shared that the technique becomes more and more effective. He mentions people have used the practice not only for anxiety and stress but also for other things like alleviating cravings.

What to expect

You might find yourself feeling a little bit light-headed after doing this exercise the first few times. That is absolutely normal and will quickly pass. Dr. Weil advises not do more than four breaths at one time for the first month of practice (so follow the good doctor's advice).

Although the anti-anxiety calming effects of this exercise can be experienced immediately, the real power of this technique comes with regular daily practice. By practicing these deeper rhythms consciously, we create more effective sub-conscious patterns of breathing, therefore integrating the physiological effects into our daily lives. With enough practice, you should begin breathing more deeply without having to give it any extra thought.

When you use this technique to help you get to relax at bedtime (more on this later), some people will tell you they don't remember getting past the first set of 4-7-8 before they were sound asleep!

This is a simple method that can very effectively stop anxiety in its tracks by almost immediately creating a calm, inner peace and turning off the fight-or-flight response. It slows down your body's inflammatory response to all those stress hormones.

Try it. Thank me later.

2

GENERAL ANXIETY DISORDER

*W*hat is General Anxiety Disorder (GAD)?

GAD can be a long-term condition that causes someone to feel anxious about a wide range of situations and issues rather than one specific event.

People with GAD feel anxious most days and often struggle to remember the last time they felt relaxed. As soon as one anxious thought is resolved, another may appear about a different issue.

GAD can cause both psychological and physical symptoms. These will vary from person to person, but include any or several of the following items.

- Restlessness
- A sense of dread
- Feeling constantly *"on edge"*
- Difficulty concentrating
- Irritability

- Dizziness
- Tiredness
- A noticeably strong, fast or irregular heartbeat (palpitations)
- Muscle aches and tension
- Trembling or shaking
- Dry mouth
- Excessive sweating
- Shortness of breath
- Stomach ache
- Feeling sick
- Headache
- Pins and needles
- Difficulty falling or staying asleep (insomnia)

Anxiety Triggers

If you're anxious because of a specific phobia or because of panic disorder, you'll usually know the cause. For example, if you have claustrophobia (fear of confined spaces), you know that being confined in a small space will trigger your anxiety.

However, if you suffer with GAD, you may not always know the cause of your anxiousness. Not knowing the triggers for your anxiety can intensify it and you may start to worry that there's no solution.

People suffering with GAD may also find that they are more prone to other anxiety related issues like hypochondria, panic attacks, etc. This is something I suffered through; it took quite some time before I figured out how to take back control of my life.

My experience

Given the fairly constant chronic nature of the symptoms, a lot of people may not even know they have GAD. I was certainly in the camp of, *"I feel fine. Sometimes I may be a little stressed, but otherwise I'm fine."*

The problem was that I *wasn't* fine. My body was constantly in fight-or-flight mode. This is incredibly fatiguing on both body and mind.

To combat my first symptoms, I started using caffeine to keep my awake and focused. This worked for a short time, and then ceased to have an effect. I tired using more caffeine, but there's only so many cups of coffee you can drink in a day before you realize that enough is enough.

When I decided to give up caffeine and fix myself is when I realized how broken I was.

Without coffee, I struggled to get out of bed in the morning, despite making sure I had eight to ten hours sleep. My brain refused to work. I couldn't remember words; I couldn't learn any new information or retain anything. I felt depressed, anxious and helpless all of the time.

While all that sounds like great fun, what has it got to do with GAD?

Well, I genuinely believe there are thousands of people out there who are living with GAD and masking it with caffeine, nicotine and other substances just to get through the day.

What Can You Do to Overcome It?

GAD is slightly different than other panic disorders in that it's not a single event that happens periodically; rather, it's an ongoing state. As such, the methods used to overcome it need to be used on an ongoing basis as well. Luckily, this is not difficult.

My experience of GAD manifested itself as agoraphobia, hypochondria, and subsequently panic attacks. Yours will probably be something different. Regardless of the symptoms, the techniques to overcome it will be the same and the results you can get from it will be just as powerful!

Coherent breathing

Coherent breathing is simply the practice of slowing your breathing to a rate of five breaths per minute. It's as simple as counting to five on the inhale and counting to five on the exhale. You simply repeat this for five minutes. Easy, huh?

This simple and powerful technique will calm your nervous system in a more prolonged way. What you'll find compared to other breathing techniques (like the 4-7-8 breath) is that they are very instant and noticeable in their effects. Coherent breathing has the same effects, but it happens in a slightly different way. You'll find it still delivers that calming effect, but it is more subtle so it leads to a longer period of calm and relaxation. These attributes make it perfect for dealing with GAD as the effects of the breathing tie in nicely with the symptoms of the disorder.

As a quick overview:

- Breath in through your nose for the count of five.
- Breath out through your mouth for the count of five.
- Repeat for five minutes.

This exercise is best practiced two to three times daily for a least a week. If you really try it for a week and decide it's not for you, then fine; there are a number of other techniques in this book you can try. But I've seen this simple exercise dissipate issues like GAD not only for myself, but for others. I really believe it's worth a try.

Have you got a spare 15 minutes a day to get rid of your anxiety? I thought so. Give it a go!

3

ANXIETY ATTACKS & PANIC ATTACKS

*M*y last book was all about these suckers, and for good reason; they're incredibly pervasive in modern society. It's thought that over four million Americans suffer from panic attacks according to the National Institutes of Mental Health. That's about five percent of the adult population. A lot of researchers feel that number is a low estimate, as so many people who experience panic or anxiety attacks never receive the proper diagnosis and just "live" with it, despite the debilitating issues that it brings.

What are Panic Attacks versus Anxiety Attacks?

First, I want to be clear that there is a distinction; anxiety and panic are not the same thing. They are very closely related, but they are not identical. Many of the symptoms associated with both are similar, hence why they are sometimes grouped together.

Panic attacks are very real, very nasty, and can be incredibly emotionally draining. Many people who experience their first panic attack find themselves in emergency rooms or at doctors' offices, expecting to hear the worst about their health.

Many of the symptoms of a panic attack can lead people to feel as if they are having a heart attack as a tight chest and heart palpitations are common effects of a panic attack. Some people might feel the fear that they'll "lose control" of themselves and could do something humiliating in front of other people.

Panic attacks are generally considered to be sudden and extremely intense. They don't always have a reason for occurring and tend to last no more than 10-30 minutes. Sometimes attacks can occur in succession, so can give the feeling of a continuous state of panic.

After an attack has happened, the person tends to feel stressed and on-edge about the potential of another attack.

Sadly, many people don't seek help for panic attacks and related conditions like agoraphobia. This is especially heart breaking because panic and other anxiety disorders are very treatable and respond well to simple, short-term therapy options.

Thankfully, more and more people are heading to doctors and specialists about this, though some people are initially frustrated. When people find out they don't have a life-threatening condition (like a heart attack), this news might actually *increase* their anxiety and frustration as they start to think, *"Well, if I am physically OK, what happened to me? I know something happened, even if I can't quite explain it right now. What's wrong with me?"*

People that are undiagnosed with panic attacks or a panic disorder can find that they bounce from one doctor to the next for months or even years without anyone being able to point to one thing and say, *"This is the problem."*

Anxiety attacks tend to be ongoing, ever present feelings. Anxiety attacks are usually associated with specific events or fears. For example, if someone is worrying about an upcoming test, they might go over all the negative points in their head, over and over, increasing their stress and worrying about the event. This seemingly self-perpetuating condition can be classed as anxiety. While it's generally not as extreme in its symptoms compared to panic disorders, it can still have an extremely detrimental effect on someone's life if they let it get out of hand.

Luckily, awareness for these types of disorders are growing in the medical community so people suffering are more likely than ever to be diagnosed and successfully treated.

Symptoms

The symptoms can really range from person to person, but the most common panic attacks last only a few minutes, though they can last longer. Panic attack symptoms are:

- A racing and pounding heartbeat.
- Light-headedness and dizziness.

- A feeling of not being able to catch your breath.
- Chest pains or a heavy feeling in the chest.
- Flushes or chills.
- Feeling of terror.
- Feeling of losing control.
- Feeling a fear of a stroke or something that will lead to disability.
- Feeling a fear of dying.
- Feeling a fear of going crazy.
- Tingling in the hands, feet, legs or arms.
- Jumpiness with trembling or twitching muscles.
- Sweaty palms.
- Flushed face.

Typical symptoms of anxiety attacks are:

- Feeling generally anxious, uneasy or nervous.
- Feeling easily irritated.
- Feeling doubtful of your own self-worth and self-confidence.
- Feeling faint or light-headed.
- Feeling disconnected from your current situation.
- An on-going feeling of hopelessness.
- Heavy breathing.
- Constant crying or the feeling of needing to cry.
- Muscle pain or soreness not related to physical activity.
- Twitching, trembling or shaky feelings in your limbs.
- Sweaty palms.
- Trouble concentrating or remembering things.

- A feeling of wanting to escape from your place or situation.
- A continuing focus on upsetting events in your own and other people's lives.
- Repeating negative conversations in your head.

There are, of course, a number of different disorders within the brackets of panic and anxiety. These disorders range from mild to severe, from sporadic to constant. What's important to understand is that, ultimately, they all stem from the same place and they can all be treated in a similar way.

The National Institutes of Mental Health (a division of the National Institute of Health) is currently conducting a nationwide campaign to educate the general public and health care practitioners that panic and the other anxiety disorders are some of the most successfully treated psychological problems today. A history of clinical research provides us with a solid blueprint of cognitive, emotional and behavioral methods that have proven effective in helping sufferers overcome anxiety disorders.

Is this really all in my head?

Due to the very strong, physical reactions people have when experiencing a panic attack or at the pinnacle of an anxiety attack, many people believe there must be an underlying disease or disorder, not associated with panic or anxiety.

The symptoms of panic attacks are very real are due to the

body's fight-or-flight response going into overdrive. Hormones flood through the body, nerve cells fire as panic grows and the body prepares for the worst.

This is usually in conjunction with extremely negative thoughts, such as:

"I think I'm losing control."

"I'm going crazy."

"I'm having a heart attack."

"I'm smothering. I can't breathe."

Thoughts like these are frequent in the context of panic attacks. So don't worry, you're not alone. You're not "going crazy" and you are not losing control!

The Aftermath

After experiencing a panic attack or an episode of intense anxiety, people often find the tension lingers in the form of a nagging fear, such as, *"When will this happen to me again?"*

Some people become so frightened of having panic attacks (especially in public places) that they withdraw to their *"safe zones."* These areas tend to be their homes, and people can become dependent on that feeling of safety that comes with it. In fact, many people rarely leave their homes at all in fear of another attack. This fear of leaving the safe place is a condition known as agoraphobia. I struggled with it when anxiety and panic attacks started affecting me.

People with agoraphobia don't *enjoy* having their life restricted so much; it's a depressing and miserable side effect of the condition. It's the fear of having further panic attacks in public (which is a place where they don't feel safe) that keeps them stuck in their home.

The aftermath of a panic attack can be just as uncomfortable as the fear of leaving the safe place. Feelings of depression and helplessness are not uncommon. The greatest fear tends to be that the panic attack will come back again and again, making life extremely uncomfortable.

Panic attacks are not necessarily brought on by a specific circumstance. Very often, the root causes and frequent triggers remain a mystery to the person suffering. Panic attacks can come "out of the blue" but sometimes excessive stress or other negative conditions can also initiate an attack.

Treatments

Today, panic attacks, anxiety and agoraphobia can be treated not only easily, but also successfully with a range of cures. Overcoming panic and anxiety means you no longer have attacks. It also means that you no longer have the initial symptoms that lead you to have a panic attack — the underlying cause and symptoms must be gone before we say that someone has *"overcome"* a panic disorder.

Cognitive behavioral therapy

Cognitive behavioral therapy (or CBT) is a relatively new treatment for panic disorders and agoraphobia that has been shown to be very successful. Instead of using traditional analysis-based therapy, practitioners employ new CBT methods to focus on the present problem with panic and work through how to eliminate it.

CBT has been referred to as the "how to" therapy due to it's focus on "how to" eliminate the thoughts and feelings that lead to panic and anxiety.

If you experience panic and agoraphobia, you're not *"crazy"* and you don't need to be in therapy for extended periods of time. Sessions will depend on the severity of the condition and, of course, your willingness as the patient to actively participate in the treatment.

When a person with a panic disorder is motivated to practice and try new techniques, that person is actively changing the way their brain responds. If you change the way your brain responds in a structured positive way, anxiety and panic will continue to dissipate. As time progresses, the strategies you use against it will become stronger and a complete absence of panic disorders can be achieved.

If you're in the position to see a therapist that practices CBT, I would definitely recommend it. However, you don't *need* a therapist to overcome panic attacks. You can do it with breathing exercises, the right supplements and patience.

That's how I overcame my situation, and you can, too.

Self-controlled breathing techniques

There are two main ways to tackle panic attacks with breathing:

1. Stopping a panic attack when you are having one.
2. Stopping a panic attack from occurring again.

The first tactic you need to consider is how do you stop a panic attack when you're having one. It's a powerful thought. You turn off your body's fight-or-flight response. And what's the simplest way to do that? I would recommend using the 4-7-8 breath mentioned earlier.

Just as a quick reminder to save you scrolling back through the pages, here's how you do it.

1. Sit comfortably in a straight-back position.
2. Place the tip of your tongue on the ridge of your gums, just behind your front teeth.
3. Expand your diaphragm and slowly inhale through your nose for a count of **four**.
4. Hold your breath for another count of **seven**.
5. Open your mouth slightly and exhale for **eight** counts, contracting your diaphragm.
6. Repeat this cycle four times.

If you follow this process, you should feel that your panic attack stops, or at the very least lessens significantly. If the feelings of panic persist after running through the process, simply repeat for another four rounds or until a feeling of calm has been reached. This is the technique I used success-fully to get my life back from panic attacks and it continues to be useful to this day.

To address the second way to lessen the impact of your panic and anxiety (*how do you stop attacks from occurring again*), it's simple: *a daily breathing practice.*

The idea behind a daily breathing practice is that your body becomes used to feeling calm and relaxed. Because of this, there will less likelihood of your body going into fight-or-flight mode (therefore, less likelihood of a panic attack occurring).

It doesn't take long to learn or feel the positive effects. It's very easy and there are many options. My two favorites are both yogic breathing exercises that I describe below. (Don't worry, you don't need to know how to bend your legs behind your back to do them!) They're simple and effective tools to use to alleviate the fear of having a panic attack ever again.

Alternate nostril breathing

This yogic breathing technique promotes deep relaxation through the balance of the right and left sides of the brain as the nervous system is calmed.

- **Sit down with both of your legs crossed or propped up on a pillow.** You can also kneel down next to the bed. Feel free to use blankets or any other object that can provide you with adequate support.

- **Rest your left hand over your left thigh.** The fingers on your right hand should be extended as if you are trying to wave at someone. Bend your middle and index fingers so that they curl inside your palm.
- **Put your thumb on the side of your nose and slightly touch your nostrils.** When you touch your nostrils, be careful not to be constricting. The idea is to limit airflow temporarily to one nostril.
- **Take a deep inhale and then exhale.** Close off your right nostril using your thumb. Breathe in through your left nostril for four seconds. When you reach the peak of that breath, you should close off your left nostril using your ring finger.
- **For four counts, hold this position to retain the breath.** Release your right nostril and breathe out for four seconds.
- **Then, take a deep breath for four seconds through your right nostril.** Just like what you did before, close it off, hold the position and retain your breath for four seconds. Release your left nostril as you breathe out fully for four seconds. Take a deep breath through your left nostril and repeat the entire cycle.

You can do this breathing technique as often as you want. When you're done, you will continue on with your day in a more relaxed state.

Deep throat breathing

This breathing technique also comes from yoga. It relaxes the body and calms the mind. You'll probably want to be in bed or on a comfortable floor for this one. I'd recommend trying it just before you go to sleep to aid in a restful night.

- **Simply lie down on your back with your legs** positioned as wide as your hips. Relax your arms at your sides and close your eyes.
- **Breathe in deeply through your nose and breathe out through your mouth.** With every breath you take, you should fill your lungs totally. Similarly, with every exhale you do, breathe out completely.
- **After taking three deep breaths,** inhale through your nose for four counts while constricting the back of your throat a bit. This way, you will feel as if you are breathing through a straw at the back of your throat as well as filling your lungs with air.
- **You should notice the sound of your breath mimicking the sound of waves that come in and out.** This sound is actually very helpful in making you fall asleep. You can compare it to the soft snore of a baby.
- **Hold your breath at the top for four seconds as you silently observe your feelings.** You should aim to feel relaxed and full. Breathe out through your nose for four seconds while constricting your throat a little.
- Once your lungs have released all the air, you should begin to fill them again.
- Take a deep breath for six seconds and hold it for another six seconds.
- Finally, breathe out for six seconds.

- Repeat this breathing process, adding two seconds more for every cycle.

After you reached your maximum capacity of breathing and holding, you can begin taking away a couple of seconds at a time. So, if twelve seconds is the maximum amount of time that you can do, your next round should be down to ten seconds. Continue subtracting two seconds every time, so the next round is eight seconds and so on.

When you reach four seconds, you can release everything and return to normal breathing. Now that you have relaxed your mind and body, you can have a peaceful sleep and wake up feeling refreshed and rejuvenated.

You can do these exercises in the morning, before bed or anywhere else in between. The key point is that you need to do them every day. You should notice your tendency for anxiety and panic attacks diminishing over time the longer you use them.

4

PHOBIAS

*W*hat Are Phobias?

Phobias affect pretty much everyone. They can affect people in a small way, such as the classic "phobia of public speaking," which is one that most people don't have to deal with on a day-to-day basis. Unfortunately, phobias can also affect people in big way, like with agoraphobia where people struggle to leave their house. Phobias such as these can be debilitating but they are very treatable.

And if you have a phobia, don't think you're strange or different because of it. There are phobias for pretty much everything. If you can imagine it, someone has a phobia of it. Like Aurophobia- the fear of gold. Quadraphobia – the fear of the number four and it's related cousin, Quintaphobia- the fear of the number five.

Personally, I struggled with agoraphobia shortly after I started having panic attacks. I was constantly terrified of the thought of leaving my house in case I had an attack. So I stayed indoors - *for about three months.*

I lost my job because I couldn't go to work. I alienated my friends, as I wouldn't go out to see anyone. I was miserable and bored because I felt trapped without anything to do. When I did manage to get out, I had this really overpowering feeling that I would fall *up*, into the sky, as if I was in any open space.

This whole period of my life was about as fun as it sounds and one day, I'd had enough! I started researching everything I could on phobias and how to fix them. Within a couple of weeks, I was functioning again. I could leave the house. I could play football in a big open field without the fear I might fall up into the sky. I could go out with friends without worrying about being far away from home.

It was awesome. It didn't take long and, once I figured out what to do, it wasn't difficult either. More to come on other steps you can take in the chapters ahead.

Symptoms

The main distinction I want to draw here is that phobias and "fear" are not necessarily the same thing.

You can "fear" a tiger. You wouldn't want to become its lunch, for instance. But you don't necessarily have a phobia of them. The thought of being eaten by a tiger is probably not a thought that bothers you daily.

A phobia is described as "an overwhelming and debilitating fear of an object, place, situation, feeling or animal." Phobias are much more pronounced than fears. They occur when a person has an exaggerated or unrealistic sense of danger about a situation or object.

If a phobia becomes very severe, a person may organize their life around avoiding the thing that's causing them anxiety, as was my experience.

Typical symptoms for someone with a phobia or thinking about the "object" of a phobia would be:

- An unsteadiness, lightheaded and dizziness.
- A feeling of nausea.
- Sweating.
- Trembling or shaking.
- An upset stomach.
- An increased heart rate and palpitations.
- A shortness of breath.

All unpleasant but all very similar to the other responses we've been discussing. This is because these symptoms are caused by the same fight-or-flight response as panic attacks and other anxiety disorders.

The good news is it means phobias are just as treatable with similar tools and techniques.

Treatment

There are a few ways of overcoming a phobia. Most of them

are terribly unpleasant, but effective. If a phobia is something that is effecting your life negatively, working towards resolving it might be challenging, but very much worth it. This is a brief chapter on some of the options available to you if you don't know where to start.

Exposure therapy

The traditional method for treating a phobia would be to use exposure therapy. This is exactly how it sounds. You gradually and repeatedly expose yourself to what you fear in a safe, controlled way. During this process, the idea is that you'll learn to ride out the anxiety and fear until it passes.

The conventional wisdom is that through repeated experiences facing your fear, you (and your body) will begin to realize that the worst isn't going to happen. With each exposure, you feel more confident and in control. The phobia begins to lessen and lose its power.

Successfully facing fears in this way takes preparation, repetition and patience. It's not an overnight thing. But it might be something to consider.

Visualizing and relaxing

This is similar to exposure therapy, but with one main bonus — you can do it from the comfort of your chair!

1. Imagine what scares you; really visualize it as clearly as you can.

2. Feel the fear and emotions build (uncomfortable part, but important).
3. While visualizing yourself experiencing your phobia and feeling the emotions, do a calming breathing exercise, such as the 4-7-8 breath.
4. Repeat 3-4 times and notice if your fear is lessened by the end.

This technique has all the benefits of traditional exposure therapy, but results should come faster. It's efficacy is predicated on the subject really trying to visualize and feel the scary emotions as much as possible. It's not always the easiest to do, but ultimately it can really be worth it in order to get rid of your phobia.

Other options

Now there are other exercises that might not completely alleviate your phobias, but they should (at the very least) lessen them somewhat. Some are outside the scope of this book, but I would like to draw your attention to one that might help: EFT, which stands for Emotional Freedom Technique.

It's a very powerful and simple tool to work with any unwanted thought patterns or physical symptoms of anxiety and other disorders. It's basically a process of tapping on key points in your body while reciting positive self-talk. Sounds strange, I know. But it's remarkably simple and effective.

5

NATURAL REMEDIES

*D*ISCLAIMER: *What is discussed in these next pages is focused mainly around natural and over-the-counter supplements; it is always advised to speak to your doctor before trying any of them.*

Are There Natural Anti-Anxiety Relief Methods That Can Help?

Anti-anxiety supplements are becoming increasingly popular as an alternative to anxiety medications, and can be more immediate than therapy or other long term treatments. The problem with this "solution" is that there are thousands of them. Pretty much every major natural medicine company has developed their own product or blend for the anxiety market. There are a couple of problems with "solutions" like these.

First, according to studies, most natural anxiety medicines are ineffective. Another issue is when given that there are so many products on the market, it can be really hard to know which supplements are likely to work and which ones aren't.

One thing to bear in mind is that natural supplements can be a great choice for those that want to consider other means of treatment. But you need to recognize they're still only a temporary treatment. Using everything else in this book, you can learn how to cope with anxiety better and take steps toward curing it forever. But in the meantime, supplements can be great for making you feel like yourself again!

Also, know that there isn't as much difference between medication and natural supplements as you might first have thought. The stronger a supplement, the more likely it is going to have side effects or risks (which is true of anything that changes your body chemistry). Also, as mentioned before, not all anxiety is treated in the same way. Panic attacks may require a different type of treatment than GAD, for example, so what works for one person may not work for you — being smart about your options is important and why you are reading this book!

There are a million and one things you could take and a million people telling you that their product is the best and most effective. I'm going to tell you what worked for me and what's been shown to work in clinical conditions.

The big two

The two remedies I think are really worth talking about are; **Rhodiola Rosea** & **L-Theanine.** There are a number of studies on each of them, expounding their effectiveness as well as plenty of anecdotal evidence and -out of everything I've tried -they seem to be the most effective.

Rhodiola Rosea

Rhodiola Rosea is an herb that can prove to be really effective for treating anxiety. It's more commonly taken as an anti-depressant; however, many anti-depressants are also recommended for people who suffer from anxiety as they will both work on similar neurotransmitters and pathways.

This herb grows in cold regions and can go by many other names, including: arctic root, golden root, rose root, Aaron's rod and king's crown. All of these refer to the same small plant with yellow flowering stalks.

In Russia, Scandinavia and China, Rhodiola Rosea has been traditionally collected and taken to cope with the stresses of life in extremely cold and high-altitude climates. Specifically, its key effects are on reducing fatigue, increasing sexual potency and promoting happiness.

In recent years, studies supporting its use as an antidepressant has promoted the U.S. Food and Drug Administration (FDA) to remove some products containing rhodiola rosea from the market. There were concerns around some people claiming this herb's potential as a treatment for the migraines, flu, colds, bacterial infections and even cancer, though these claims have since been proven to be false or unsupported.

Although not entirely understood, Rhodiola Rosea is

believed to have combined both stimulating and relaxing qualities in a ratio that make it effective for people suffering from depression and anxiety.

Some of the well-established effects of Rhodiola Rosea are:

- **Decreasing activity in the Sympathetic Nervous System.** Remember, the sympathetic nervous system (SNS) is what jumps into action when the fight-or-flight response is triggered by the amygdala. This results in the familiar symptoms of raising your pulse, your breathing rate and taxing your adrenal glands. Amplified activity of these is responsible for all the physical symptoms of anxiety you may have experienced, such as a rapid heartbeat, shaking, shortness of breath, dizziness and nausea.
- **Increasing activity in the Parasympathetic Nervous System Activity.** The parasympathetic nervous system (PNS) is the opposite of the SNS in that it is linked with the slowing of the body's processes rather than speeding them up. So, an increase in PNS activity would result in a calming and focusing effect.
- **Increasing Serotonin.** The hormone serotonin is the neurotransmitter associated with happiness and relaxation. A serotonin deficiency tends to be seen primarily in people with depression and anxiety conditions.
- **Increasing Memory and Focus.** Feeling unfocused and scattered due to anxiety can make the anxiety worse, particularly if you find yourself feeling

anxious in the middle of something important like a meeting or a test. Various studies have shown that Rhodiola Rosea improves both memory and focus. In a recent study using it as a supplement, subjects had to take a proofreading test and their memory and focus were measured. The results showed that subjects who took Rhodiola Rosea made 88% less mistakes compared to the control group.

- **Shortens Recovery Time After Exercise.** A common symptom of anxiety is that your heart rate tends to rise and your breathing can become more labored, similar to when you exercise for an extended period of time. Rhodiola Rosea can be effective for decreasing the amount of time it takes for your heart rate and breathing to return to normal. In another recent study of people who took Rhodiola Rosea before running 12 miles, the participants were tested in intervals. Those who had not taken Rhodiola Rosea showed elevated pulses 129% higher than a resting heart rate on average, while the pulses of those who had taken Rhodiola Rosea were only 105% higher than a resting rate.

There are some fantastic reasons to try Rhodiola Rosea and the effects can be profound. Certainly in my own life, I've seen a massive difference after using it. I continue to use it and I credit it with helping to keep my anxiety as well as panic attacks under control. It has the nice side effect of making you feel happier and more motivated about life, so all in all, it's a big thumbs up from me!

Should you use Rhodiola Rosea?

Ultimately, it's cheap, safe and has proven to be effective for hundreds of years. I would definitely suggest picking some up and trying it. If it doesn't work for you, that's fine. There are hundreds of other things to try, but it might be the most effective supplement you ever take to combat anxiety.

Theanine

Theanine is a common compound found mainly in green or black tea. It's a widely available supplement and can be a powerful aid in relieving anxiety. Theanine works to boost your body's functioning in a natural and effective way.

It was originally discovered when experiments with green tea lead to its extraction. Interestingly, black tea can contain as much or sometimes more Theanine as green tea as both green and black teas come from the same plant, *Camellia sinensis*. The only difference is that black tea is treated by heat and sometimes fermentated before its dried.

Seemingly, it also acts to boost brain dopamine, one of the "feel good" neurotransmitters. This could be the main reason most people report feelings of *well-being* and a *mental focus* when they take Theanine.

Is Theanine effective in treating anxiety?

There has been some research into this and while there are no conclusive *clinical* studies on this, many people (including myself) have seen that it does help relieve their anxiety. It can also have profound effects on improving sleep.

There are a number of interesting studies showing that Theanine can increase alpha-wave activity in the brain, where alpha waves are indicators of a "resting" brain state. Most of these studies were not performed with subjects suffering from anxiety; however, it is usually the case that people who are prone to anxiety tend to naturally have less alpha waves and more beta wave activity (which are commonly associated with alertness and attention).

Other studies have found that Theanine helped to decrease the stress response in people put into a stressful situation under experimental conditions. These studies were not performed on anxiety sufferers, but any reduction in stress or improvement in stress management will likely help to combat and manage anxiety for someone that is.

Can I just drink a cup of tea?

As I am a British person, you'll not be surprised to hear that drinking a cup of tea would be my preferred option for any sort of treatment. Unfortunately, while drinking tea will certainly give you a small boost of Theanine, the amount isn't standardized and can vary widely. Expected dosages can range anywhere from 5 mg for a cup of ordinary tea (hot or iced, it makes no difference), up to 46 mg in a cup of high quality gourmet tea.

So, while it's not ideal, yes, you can just drink a cup of tea to get your Theanine. As mentioned, black tea contains Theanine, too, but the main difference is nothing to do with if the tea is green or black; it's how young the tea leaves are at harvest. Theanine tends to be found in the highest concentrations in the buds and in the young leaves of the tea plant.

Due to the additional expense of harvesting these teas, they tend to be more expensive. Teas like Matcha, Sencha and Gyokuro can be many times more expensive than your typical cup of tea. Oolong and Darjeeling teas are other types of "gourmet" teas that are likely to have a high concentration of Theanine, due to them being harvested from young tea plants.

This still leaves the question of how much Theanine should you take daily.

How much to take?

Theanine has been shown to have therapeutic benefits with dosages ranging between 50-200 mg. Given that amount, you're going to have to drink five to ten cups of normal tea to get the same dosage of Theanine as taking one small capsule. For me, this is no problem as I would consider five cups as a minimum for a day, but I appreciate this isn't normal for anyone outside of Briton.

This is where supplements are useful. A small pack of Theanine can be had for around $10 and will last you a couple of months. Most of the dosages tend to be standardised at 100 mg per capsule so you can determine exactly how much Theanine is right for you using a daily "testing" process.

Start of with 100 mg and see how you handle it. If you like

what you feel, maybe try a bit more; if you don't, back off on the dosages a little bit. According to the FDA, dosages up to 250 mg per day are considered safe, and for anyone I know that has used it, a higher dose than that is not necessary.

Theanine does have a relatively short half-life (meaning your body metabolizes it in approximately 2.5 – 4.5 hours), but certainly from my experiences, a single dose in the morning is enough for the entire day.

There's loads of different types! Which one do I buy!???

Theanine is an amino acid, although it doesn't form part of any protein. Like all amino acids, Theanine comes in two mirror image shapes: The "L" and the "D." You'll probably see it sold as L-Theanine versus D-Theanin. The former is the active version and D-theanine has no effect at all on your brain. (So, *L-Theanine* is the one you want!)

But, you might see some products called just "Theanine," without the "L." This happens when Theanine is synthesized in a laboratory, the result is a mix of L-Theanine (which we want) and D-Theanine (which doesn't interest us). Separating out just the L-Theanine adds an additional expense to the process. Many manufacturers may cut corners, and just use the mixture as it is.

The company uses a patented procedure of fermentation that mimics the way Theanine is produced naturally in tea leaves. Because of this special process, it's about as close to "naturally produced Theanine" as you're likely to find.

While this is all very wonderful, it's incredibly expensive to actually extract pure L-Theanine from tea leaves. As a result, most of the commercially available L-Theanine is not extracted in the same way. If you really don't mind spending a little bit more money to ensure the purity and quality of the L-Theanine you're getting, just look for a supplement that uses Suntheanine.

Having said that, L-Theanine from any other reputable company may also be pure and high quality. The only thing to be conscious of is that cheaper brands will tend not to take any effort to ensure the purity and ratio of L-Theanine and D-Theanine, as it will be much less expensive to produce, so you can't be certain how much you are really taking.

Should I try theanine?

Theanine seems to be one of the more helpful supplements you could take for anxiety. The worst risk is that it might not help you much or at all. It won't have the same powerful effect as some pharmaceutical medications, but it's not as risky, either.

In my experience, if you try Theanine, you'll to be able to function properly without feeling sedated. You won't face the risk of withdrawal or rebound anxiety if you stop taking it.

Theanine can be a fantastic supplement to help alleviate some of the symptoms of anxiety and can form a solid component as part of your self-treatment.

Is there anyone who shouldn't use Theanine?

Theanine has been studied extensively under lab conditions in both toxicology and clinical studies. There don't seem to be any reports of adverse effects in almost 50 years of use by the general population or in any of the lab studies. The only potential side effect that has appeared over the years is a headache, but that has been report to only occur with very high doses.

L-Theanine has been approved by the FDA as a supplement in the US in doses up to 250 mg. It also has been designated as GRAS (generally recognized as safe). There are a couple of things to bear in mind, though.

If you're pregnant or breast-feeding, check with your doctor first.

This should go without saying, but I'm going to say it anyway: if you are taking prescribed medication of any form, weather it's for anxiety for not, then please make sure you discuss any supplements you are thinking about using with your doctor first.

My main reservation in saying anyone can try it come with diagnosed depression or if you are prone to episodes of depression. You need to be <u>very</u> cautious about taking *anything* that increases GABA levels in your brain.

GABA

If you're suffering from anxiety, a boost in GABA levels in your brain will have a dramatic impact. GABA is a neuro-transmitter found naturally in your brain and low levels seem to be very closely linked with some types of anxiety. In this case, it makes sense that you would want to increase your GABA levels if you want to reduce your anxiety.

Taking Theanine can be a cheap and effective way to increase GABA levels. Theanine doesn't just boost GABA, it also has the synergistic effect of toning down some of the stimulating neurotransmitters that make you anxious. You might be thinking, and rightly so, *"If GABA is so good, why don't I just take some of that?"* Unfortunately, it's not always as easy as that.

Some people have had great results from taking a GABA supplement. The main problem is that it doesn't cross the blood-brain barrier very effectively; this means most of the GABA in the supplement doesn't end up getting where you need it to go — and we have no way to measure how much truly gets absorbed. Due to this, it can be very difficult to regulate your brain levels of GABA by a direct supplement.

Now there are some super-fancy GABA pills out there that use really interesting techniques to overcome this, such as one company attached the GABA molecule to a liposome (molecule of fat) to enable it to be more effectively digested and absorbed. The only problem is, it's very expensive. If you've got money to burn, check it out. If not, maybe Theanine could be the answer.

Interestingly, Theanine does cross the blood-brain barrier quite well. It tends to have the same effect as raising GABA in your brain, so it can be a very quick and easy way to achieve the same thing.

. . .

Synergistic Supplements

Like any supplement derived from plants, tea may provide additional ingredients that we have not yet identified. Some of these ingredients may work with Theanine to enhance its effects.

The main one we do know about is caffeine. In tea, it seems to have a very positive interaction with Theanine and will be much less likely than coffee to give you the jitters.

Unfortunately, caffeine might not be great for most people with anxiety. I certainly saw a drastic improvement in my anxiety and panic attacks when I eliminated caffeine from my diet. Let's go into more detail in the next chapter.

6

AVOIDING CAFFEINE

While this section looks at which supplements work well for reducing anxiety, an important thing to remember is there are some things you take that may have a negative impact on your anxiety.

Really annoyingly for me, caffeine turned out to be a big trigger of anxiety for me. And I learned that it's a very common trigger for inducing anxiety and panic attacks.

How Do I Know If Caffeine Is Making My Anxiety Worse?

I love coffee. I have for years. I love the smell, I love the complexity of the flavor and I loved the way it woke me up in the mornings. For the past few years, my morning always started with a cup of good coffee and I'd sometimes have double espresso later on in the day if I needed an extra boost.

When I started having issues with anxiety and panic attacks, I read everything I could and learned there is a lot of evidence to suggest that caffeine can increase and sometimes even *cause* anxiety.

I obviously thought I was one of the lucky ones where that wasn't an issue, because I'd been drinking it long before any of these issues had occurred, so it couldn't have been the cause. I was obviously OK with caffeine… but after a couple of months of panic attacks and sustained anxiety, I decided to try cutting out caffeine for a couple of days to see if it made any difference — desperate times call for desperate measures.

On the first day, I had no coffee to start my morning. It was a bit more difficult to get going and I certainly yawned a few more times than I normally would have, but… I had no panic attacks and little to no anxiety.

Interesting.

So the next day, the same thing: no coffee and no anxiety.

On the third day, I decided to have my morning fix of caffeine again. It was delicious. I missed it. I missed the smell. I missed the taste. What I had not been missing was the anxiety and subsequent panic attack I had that morning.

Now I know that could have been a fluke. Correlation does not necessarily equate to causation. So I tried extending the *"No Caffeine"* experiment to two full weeks. During that time, I had no further issues with panic attacks and dramatically reduced ongoing anxiety.

At the end of the two weeks, I rewarded myself with a coffee… you can probably guess the experience. Anxiety increased and I had a panic attack within a couple of hours of drinking my cup of wonderful coffee.

I've since done my best to abstain from large doses of caffeine and it's certainly been a big driver in my reduced anxiety. Annoyingly, everything out there seems to have caffeine: headache medicine, soda drinks, even tea. Seemingly though, tea doesn't have a negative effect. I'm guessing it's due to the reduced caffeine content compared to coffee and the additional calming compounds like Theanine.

Giving Up Caffeine

Now you might be thinking, *"Wow, I'd better give up caffeine right away!"* There's a greater likelihood that you're thinking, *"There's no way I'm giving up caffeine! It can't be bad for me. I've been drinking it for years! How am I going to get through my morning without that? I'll fall asleep at my desk!..."* and so on.

Now look, I won't sugar-coat it. Going cold turkey on caffeine is up there with some of the more unpleasant experiences of my life and I would certainly like to avoid doing it again if possible. I had headaches, I felt tired, I was miserable... but I didn't have any panic attacks, so overall it was a plus.

The good news is that you can reap all the benefits of giving up caffeine cold turkey with none of the downsides. All you have to do is cut down *gradually*.

The Plan

Before you go through any of this plan, first just try a day without caffeine. That's no coffee, no tea, no soda, no energy drinks or anything else with caffeine hidden in it. If you see an improvement in your symptoms or you feel any positive benefit at all, you owe it to yourself to try and wean yourself off caffeine, even if it's only for a short time.

It's simple really. All you need to do is lower your intake of daily caffeine, a little bit at a time, over the course of a week or two.

Here, I'm going to use coffee as an example as it tends to be the most prominent source of caffeine for many people.

- **Day 1:** Just drink your normal amount of coffee.
- **Days 2 – 5:** Start blending your coffee with around 50% decaffeinated. Continue to drink that until the end of day 5.
- **Day 6:** Next, blend 25% of your regular coffee with 75% decaf for one day.
- **Day 7:** Drink only decaf coffee.

* * *

CONGRATULATIONS! You're now officially off coffee!

* * *

Now if you go through that and don't see any improvement, you're one of the lucky ones who can have caffeine without issue! Grab a cup of Joe and enjoy your morning.

If, however, you're like me or the majority of people experiencing anxiety, you'll probably have seen a marked improvement by cutting out caffeine. If that's the case, it's easier than you think to live without caffeine.

How to live without caffeine

There are a few different options to replace caffeinated drinks with to help you stick to your plan.

- Caffeine-free soft drink – They are pretty easy to find if you read the labels.
- Sparkling water – It's an acquired taste, but it's the most amazing thing! They make some naturally flavored with fruit juice and things, too.
- Decaf coffee – If you get the good brands, it tastes the same! And you can enjoy one later in the evening without it screwing with your sleep.

The only thing I haven't found a good substitute for energy drinks yet. They're basically just caffeine drinks so stick to sparkling water if you can. If not, a caffeine-free soft drink if you need that sweetness or fruit juice flavored sparkling drinks work well, too.

Other Benefits of Eliminating Caffeine

So you're still weighing whether to cut out caffeine or not. I get it. It's a hard thing to considered because it's so engrained in all of our lives.

If the thought of potentially eliminating your anxiety overnight isn't enough of a driver for you, there are a few other reasons you should consider eliminating caffeine.

Save money

That daily coffee can add up and thousands of dollars a year.

- A Grande Starbucks Latte: $3.65 a day | $26 a week | **$1,332 a year**
- 5-hour energy: $3 a day | $21 a week | **$1,095 a year**
- Home brewed coffee: $.71 a day | $5 per week | **$259 a year**
- Monster Energy Drink: $3 a day | $21 a week | **$1,095 a year**
- K-cups: $.65 a day | $4.55 a week | **$237 a year**

That's some pretty serious savings. Just think what you could do with that extra couple of grand a year!

Lower your blood pressure

Caffeine has been shown to raise your blood pressure. Cutting out caffeine can lower your blood pressure and keep your heart healthier for longer.

Better sleep

Caffeine can have a large, detrimental impact on the quality of your sleep. Drinking coffee or other caffeinated drinks too late in the day can interfere with getting to sleep as caffeine tends to stay in your system for four to six hours.

A good idea is to at least cut out caffeine after 12 noon and you should see a marked improvement in the quality of your sleep.

Better mood

Caffeine alters your mood. It's not uncommon to hear people say they're grumpy until they've had their morning coffee and they start to feel lethargic when it starts to wear off in the afternoon.

If you quit caffeine altogether, you no longer have these ups and downs. You can have sustained energy throughout the day with no crashes and no grumpiness.

Whiter and healthier teeth

It's well known that coffee and tea can stain your teeth. Energy drinks and soft drinks are just as bad and they can erode tooth enamel and can cause decay.

Eliminating them will help you towards healthier and (some would say, more importantly) whiter teeth.

Significant weight loss

Caffeinated drinks generally add empty calories to our diets that don't benefit us in any way. Many experts state that sugary beverages are a large factor in the obesity epidemic.

Look at what you could save by cutting out those caffeinated drinks.

- Quitting a "one energy drink per day" habit saves 200 calories per day, 1,400 calories a week, and **73,000 calories a year**!
- Quitting that "one Starbucks Vanilla Latte per day" would save you 250 calories per day, 1,750 calories a week, and **91,250 calories a year**!

Are you kidding me? Over 90,000 calories a year? Here's a simple tag-line: *"Cut out your vanilla Latte and get abs."*

No more jitters

One of the main side-effects people experience with caffeine is jittery or shaky hands. This could be a minor inconvenience, or a major one. Either way, quitting can steady your steady hands again and steady your progress toward a healthier self.

Lower risk of cardiac issues

Caffeine stimulates the heart muscles, causing your heart to beat with more powerful contractions. Those with underlying heart conditions can be at risk. Remember, too, that a stronger push by the muscles could relate to increased interior vessel pressures and weakening of the blood vessel walls.

Reduced risk of Type 2 Diabetes

Black coffee can actually reduce the risk of diabetes. Unfortunately, most people don't drink plain black coffee. Sugared coffee or caffeinated beverages can actually increase your risk of diabetes by up to 26%, according to the Harvard School of Public Health.

So as you can see, there are a number of benefits for cutting out caffeine. It doesn't have to be permanent and with the *Easy Quit Plan*, it doesn't even have to be hard. Try it — you owe it to yourself!

7

HELPFUL SUPPLEMENTS

*I*f you decide to try Rhodiola Rosea or Theanine, you should notice a marked improvement in your anxiety levels (meaning they decrease). If you've had success and you're interested in seeing what else is out there that may be effective, you might want to try some of the other options listed in this chapter.

Supplements can be a fantastic tool to help manage and beat anxiety, but they shouldn't be your only tool. The key is to get your anxiety manageable first and then work towards eliminating it completely, forever. That's something that will take slightly more work than taking an extra couple of vitamins in the morning, but is very achievable.

Below are the most commonly used anti-anxiety supplements, broken into their main categories and some information on the effectiveness.

Herbal Interventions

Herbal supplements are the most common type available. Many believe that the correct herbs can provide your body with the same medicinal effects as any other pharmaceutical medications, but with the additional benefit of causing fewer side effects as they are generally available over the counter. The most popular herbal supplements include:

- **Kava** - one of the most common and most scientifically studied anxiety supplements available, it's one of the few herbal supplements that has been shown in research to compare favorably to common anxiety medications. It's worth considering as a supplement to try, but do note that kava is believed to interact with alcohol and other medications. It has also been linked to liver damage, but this seems to be mainly in subjects who drink alcohol regularly.
- **Passionflower** - sometimes referred to as a watered-down version of kava, but it benefits from not having the same issues with alcohol interaction. Passionflower isn't generally thought to be powerful enough for some of the more severe anxiety disorders, but it can be a useful tool for those with manageable anxiety levels.
- **Valerian Root** - traditionally used to aid sleep, its relaxation effects translate well to anxiety. Valerian root is similar to passionflower in that it will have a noticeable effect, but it probably isn't going to be strong enough if you suffer from panic attacks. It's more useful to take the edge of a stressful day or help you getting to sleep if you're worrying about something.

There are probably thousands of other herbal supplements you could consider, but these are the only few with any sort of track record and success. Herbal teas, like chamomile and peppermint, might also give you some results, but beware that results may largely be a placebo.

Vitamins and Other Supplements

Vitamin and alternative supplements are becoming more and more popular as a potential treatment for anxiety. Unfortunately, there is not enough research on the benefits of supplements and their effect on anxiety levels.

Having said that, it is very well documented that a *lack* of certain vitamins may cause anxiety; it's still not proven clinically that supplementing can have significant anti-anxiety effects.

In any case, supplementing with vitamins can be good for your health regardless, so consider trying one or more of them. The most common include:

- **Magnesium** – becoming more and more popular as a treatment for anxiety, recent studies have shown that millions of people are deficient due to changes in mineral content of foods and dietary habits. As magnesium affects the health of nerves, blood cells and more, there's a good reason to believe that low magnesium levels might be a contributing factor for some anxiety symptoms. Also, it's just pretty good for your health so try it out.

- **GABA** - the chief inhibitory neurotransmitter that slows things down and calms you, GABA can be purchased as a supplement. Unfortunately as I mentioned earlier, doses of the standard type of GABA supplements are not thought to be effective in passing the blood-brain barrier, so it's unlikely you'll notice a strong effect. You can take a GABA derivative called Phenibut, but this supplement has addiction potential with side effects, so I wouldn't really recommend going near it without doing your own extensive research.

- **5-HTP** - popular for a while with people trying to treat their anxiety and depression, it helps the body synthesize both serotonin and melatonin (both are calming and feel-good chemicals within the brain). There have a number of studies extolling the benefits of 5-HTP, but most haven't been executed well. The results should be taken with a pinch of salt. Regardless, many people swear by it so it might work for you, too.

- **Melatonin** - one of the key hormones that induces sleep, it's pumped into the brain before bedtime and helps you to relax. Thankfully, it's available as a dietary supplement. Due to its efficacy and potential inhibition of natural Melatonin production, some countries require a prescription for Melatonin. There haven't been that many studies that have looked specifically as melatonin's effect on anxiety, but again, many people to refer to it as one of their "go to" supplements.

- **B-Vitamins** - the most common vitamin on the

market, all B-vitamins can have an effect on anxiety. B-vitamins are key building blocks of the nervous system, hence why studies indicate that supplementing with B-vitamins could also improve anxiety symptoms.

Different vitamins will be more effective for different people. It's dependent on your diet, environment and your genetics. However, most vitamins are very unlikely to have any side effects when taking in amounts as recommended by health agencies such as the FDA, so while you should still discuss it with your doctor before using any vitamin supplements, you might consider trying some and seeing what benefits you get from them.

Homeopathic Alternatives

Well, call me a sceptic, but I haven't seen much that proves homeopathy works... like, at all. I haven't spoken to a single person that has had success with it.

In fact, there's very little evidence that homeopathic medicine has any effect, and most of the beliefs surrounding homeopathy go in direct opposition to modern science. Not that this is necessarily a bad thing (as the established science lore of old was that the earth was flat), so I'm happy to be proved wrong if it does come good.

Ultimately, homeopathic medicine doesn't seem to have any risks, so you can research various methods to see if they suit your needs.

8

OTHER SOLUTIONS

*B*reathing exercises and natural supplements in and of themselves can resolve anxiety issues for most people. They're incredibly powerful and that's why I wanted to write a book on them to help as many people as possible and share my experiences with what worked for me.

But what other options do you have?

If you don't fancy doing any breathing exercises or you're not keen on taking supplements, what other options are open to you for treating your anxiety?

Drugs

In the western world, pharmaceuticals seem to be the most popular choice. I really don't agree with the prevalence of drugs to treat panic, anxiety and associated disorders, but seemingly they are the go-to solution for many people.

I've mentioned a few times in this book to refer to your

doctor if you're thinking about taking any supplements, making diet changes, etc. I think it's important to have a relationship with you doctor and hopefully they can be open to other methods of treatment, not just drugs.

If you'd like to find a doctor that would be open to other methods of treatments, there are a few lists that people are building to help everyone choose a doctor that's right for them. Effectively, you want to find a functional medicine doctor. Luckily, there is an institute for that and they have a database you can search! You can find it at:

https://www.functionalmedicine.org/practitioner_search.aspx?id=117

Similarly, many people in the Paleo and Bulletproof "diet space" are turning to physicians that are more open to alternative therapies. You can find guides and lists here as well as other websites, I'm sure:

https://blog.bulletproof.com/bulletproof-doctor/

http://paleo.com.au/paleo-professionals/

http://paleononpaleo.com/paleo-doctors/

Ultimately, I'm not here to tell you to sack your doctor. I'm not here to tell you that positive thinking is going to cure cancer or anything like that. I'm here to tell you that you can make huge changes in your own heath without the need of a doctor.

Yes, if you get sick, go and see your doctor. Yes, if you can't resolve your anxiety with the steps in this book, go and see your doctor, but please don't just go on drugs because it feels like an easy way out. It's not, I promise you.

Diet

"You are what you eat." We've all heard it. It's usually a well-meant comment from someone trying to steer you away from chips and a burger toward something a bit more green and healthy.

I used to dismiss this, especially in my younger years. I thought I could eat what I wanted (usually a big bowl of pasta) and be fine. And that was the case... for a while.

A lot's changed since then and I am not the same person I was. I'm up early every day improving myself and working towards big goals, but at the time, this lazy mentality made sense to me.

The point is, when I was young and had lost my job, I got into a routine of sleeping a lot, waking up, eating a big bowl of pasta and then I would feel tired, zoned out and uninspired for the rest of the day.

I was sleeping for 12-13 hours a day and I was still tired all the time. What's that about? Unsurprisingly, this "life without any goals" happened to be around the time anxiety and depression first visited me. Coincidence? I think not.

I found a stark change in my energy and anxiety came when I found a job and started eating "better" at work. My anxiety left. My depression left. I was happier because I was healthier. As you can probably guess by the title of the section, my opinion on the matter is pretty resolute: *WHAT YOU EAT AFFECTS YOUR MOOD!*

There are many studies on how gut bacteria affect your mood and there are many studies on how different foods effect how you feel.

As a simple example, what happens when you eat a big lunch? I'm talking a couple of sandwiches or maybe some pasta, a fizzy drink and a chocolate cookie or two to finish. Now tell me, how did you feel about an hour after that?

Did you feel like you were about to fall asleep and you couldn't think quite as clearly? Did you feel a bit slow and lethargic for the rest of the day? Most likely. (If not, you're some sort of medical anomaly and you could make good money selling your body to science.)

This is just a really simple illustration as to how food can immediately affect your mind and physiology. It's not too much of a stretch then, if this extra bit of sugar at lunch can affect you so drastically that eating a sub-optimal diet can contribute to other things over the long term, namely, anxiety and panic attacks.

We already know that excess carbohydrates cause obesity (don't worry, this isn't turning into a diet book). With the global rise in obesity, we're seeing a strong correlation with a rise in neurodegenerative diseases such as Alzheimer's, which a number of scientists have called to be relabeled as Type 3 diabetes as it results from resistance to insulin in the brain.

Anyway, what science is saying then, is that excess carbohydrates in vast quantities over a period of years can cause serious damage in the body and mind.BUT... the good news is that there is *always* something you can do. The answer seems to be eating a lower carbohydrate and a higher, healthy fat diet.

Why is this important, you ask? We're starting to see strong evidence for healthy fats improving cognitive function in patients with Alzheimer's.

If that statement alone doesn't excite you, the same concept is being applied in other areas of medicine. There's quite a number of scientists getting really excited about the fact that a low carb, high fat diet (called a "ketogenic" diet) seems to have a fairly profound effect on inflammation in the body as well as a whole heap of other beneficial stuff, too.

I tried going on a ketogenic diet for a month. And I had zero panic attacks. Then I started eating carbs again and they started to come back.

I've also experimented with eliminating caffeine as I mentioned. (Well, coffee anyway. I'm British so there's no way I'm going to stop drinking tea.) I have had some pretty profound results with my changes. *No more caffeine = No more anxiety.*

Now I don't want this chapter to be a pitch for a low-carb lifestyle as you'll find endless books and blogs proclaiming it to be the best thing since sliced bread (pun intended). What I wanted to show you was that what you eat can really effect how you feel and perform. So when I say try giving up caffeine for 30 days and watch your anxiety lessen, I know it works.

This entire chapter is about showing you that. What you put into your body makes a big difference on your anxiety and panic response also.

So, eat better and feel better because of it!

Exercise

If there's one thing on which the medical community can agree, it's that exercise is good. They can also agree that the lack of exercise is bad. Plenty of studies have shown a very strong link between a lack of physical activity the likelihood of developing an anxiety disorder. While not everyone can agree on exactly why this is, some widely agreed upon causes are:

- **Increased Stress Hormones.** When you're stressed, your body releases it's chief stress hormone, cortisol. Many studies have shown that movement and exercise help to manage cortisol levels, bringing the balance it back to normal levels in the brain. This links to what we've discussed earlier in the book. Anxiety is the outward symptom of the fight-or-flight response. When your body experiences it, it expects you to fight something or flee from it. When you do nothing, your body doesn't know what to do with itself so it ramps up the production in an effort to get you take action.

- **Unused Energy.** You were made to move, and when your body doesn't move, it can create tension. You might have noticed this in animals. Dogs are especially sensitive and you'll see that when they don't get their daily walks, they can become anxious and highly-strung. It's the same concept really. It's because they're not working out their energy, and then that turns first into physical tension and subsequently into mental tension.
- **Immune System Balance.** Exercise is also a key factor in maintaining a well-regulated immune system, as well as a healthy balance of hormones in the brain and body. Some studies suggest that inactivity can prevent these balances.

As well as these main points, there might also be secondary factors. Inactive people tend to spend less time enjoying experiences and positive experiences can be really good for alleviating anxiety. People that aren't working to improve their health can develop negative health issues that can also lead to anxiety.

Whatever the mechanism, *not* exercising is *not* good for you.

Obviously, a lack of exercise isn't the only cause of anxiety for everyone. Some people can be genetically prone to anxiety. Other people have had traumatic experiences that developed their anxiety symptoms. In any case, whether inactivity caused your anxiety or not, there is plenty of research to say that exercise can be one of the best ways to manage it.

So what's in it for me?

If you've not bought into avoiding the negatives that come with *not* exercising, let me try to sell you on the *benefits* instead. Exercise *alone* can be an effective treatment to severely reduce or even eliminate your anxiety. Any physical activity will help with anxiety and, the more exercise you complete, the more likely you are to see results.

I know the thought of regularly exercising for a lot of people is daunting. It's uncomfortable to think about and it may have been something you tried and failed at before. But now you've got a bigger reason to do it. You're not just running on that treadmill to get in shape for the beach, you're doing it to beat your anxiety! That's a pretty good motivator, right?

Exercising is an extremely effective method to manage your anxiety on a daily basis. For a lot of people, exercise might be the cure on it's own. For others, exercise will form part of a larger strategy for beating anxiety. At the very least, it will be a big help and you'll be fitter and healthier because of it.

Managing your anxiety is all about using tools and techniques to improve the quality of your life. Without a doubt, exercise is one of the most potent tools for that purpose. Some of the benefits you should expect to get from regularly exercising are:

- **It's Generally Healthy.** It stands to reason if you're fit and healthy, you'll be happier, right? Exactly.
- **Less Inactivity.** Makes sense really, doesn't it? If you're exercising regularly, then all the negative results of inactivity on anxiety cease to be an issue. Even if inactivity wasn't the initial cause your

anxiety, it can absolutely makes the problem worse. Regularly exercising drastically impacts the issues you might have had with inactivity.

- **More "Feel Good" Neurotransmitters.** One of the key reasons exercise works as such an effective anxiety reduction solution is due to the fact that exercise releases natural chemicals in your body and brain that have similar effects as some manmade anxiety medications. You'll find exercise releases endorphins in your brain, which act as your body's natural painkillers. Endorphins are usually released to prevent exercise from causing pain, but they also play a huge role in regulating mood (for the better) and relaxing the mind. Really, it's everything we want from medication, but side-effect free!

- **Reduction in Cortisol.** Anyone experiencing anxiety is likely to have an excess of cortisol in their body. This is due to stress that anxiety places on them. Exercise has the wonderful effect of lowering that cortisol and thus, mitigating many of the symptoms that can lead to further anxiety, like concentration problems and fatigue.

- **Better Sleep.** If you've ever exercised strenuously, you'll know that falling asleep gets a lot easier that night. Your body is tired and it needs time to rest and rebuild. As falling asleep can be something causing struggles for many anxiety sufferers, exercise can be a great natural way to induce sleep faster and to improve the quality of the sleep. Improved sleep quality will have a large impact on anyone suffering with anxiety, as your body will have time to really rest and recuperate.

And a few others...

- Less tension, stress and mental fatigue.
- A natural energy boost.
- A sense of achievement.
- Focus in life and motivation.
- Less anger or frustration.
- A healthy appetite.
- A better social life.
- Having fun!

There are a million other reasons why exercising will improve your anxiety. Exercise improves confidence. It's healthy for your body and good physical health is incredibly important for maintaining a healthy mind. It helps every aspect of your body run more efficiently and promotes balance in your body.

So what do I have to do?

When most people hear, *"Hey, you should start exercising and you'll feel great,"* they usually turn off and think, *"Yeah yeah, I've heard that before but I've never been able to stick with a routine for very long. Exercising is not for me."*

If you haven't exercised in a while, picking up the habit can be difficult... but not as difficult as living with anxiety for the rest of your life!

When you first start, it's always going to be harder before it gets easier. Your body needs to get used to pushing itself. What you'll find within a week or two is that you'll be able to work out harder, for longer, with less stress on your breathing and more feel-good endorphins being released! The good news is you don't actually need to exercise intensely. You simply need to move more.

I definitely think you should work your way up to more intense exercise. Some of the main benefits of exercise require pushing your body to adapt and change, but any movement is better than no movement. Even if it's just a 20-minute walk or you go and play some basketball once a day, you'll see a clear difference in your anxiety.

How to get started

Exercise doesn't have to be anything too strenuous. In fact, it doesn't have to feel like exercise at all. You can start by just taking a walk. The important thing is that you just get moving. Find something you feel you could stick to and then make sure you do it every day.

If walking isn't your bag, there are nearly limitless options.

- **Get a bike and ride everywhere** – I use mine to go to and home from work. It saves me a fortune in gas!
- **Play sports** – Football or basketball. Whatever your favorite sport is, get out there and play it! Have fun and start of easy.
- **Exercising at home** – There are probably hundreds of fitness channels on YouTube with workout

programs you can do at home, usually with no additional equipment. These can be really effective and best of all, they're free!

- **Running** – You don't have to try for a marathon straight out of the gate, just start with short runs up the road and back and build your stamina.
- **Lift weights** – Joining a gym can be daunting, but you don't have to jump straight into it. You can work your way up to it as you get healthier!
- **Classes at the gym** – If you're working your way towards lifting weights, a great idea is to start taking the classes that most gyms offer. These can range from circuit training, to spinning, dancing and anything else. Find one that sounds like fun and go for it!
- **Swimming** – You don't have to want to be Michael Phelps to swim. It's great exercise and it's fun. As an added bonus, the cold water exposure can help burn fat!
- **Yoga** – If you don't fancy moving about that much but still want to increase your heart rate, Yoga and stretching exercises can be a great way to do so.

Ultimately, it's just about getting moving. If you're using your muscles and getting your heart beating a little faster (even if it's a lower intensity exercise), you're having a big impact on reducing your anxiety symptoms.

How much should I exercise?

The general guideline for adults is to aim for around 150

minutes of *moderate* activity every week. This works out as an average of 30 minutes, five times a week. Initially, this might sound like a lot, but even a quick 15-minute walk can help you clear your mind and relax.

Ultimately, all your exercise will be leading up to more and more intense exercises as, the higher the intensity of your exercise, the more benefits you'll get from it and the more of a positive impact you'll see with your anxiety. As always, I would advise talking to your doctor before starting any kind exercise program - especially if you're planning on making it an intense one.

The main take away from all this is; *any exercise is better than none.*

Affirmations

Now, this might sound a bit "out-there," but just roll with me on this one for a moment. So much of depression and anxiety is centered around negative thought patterns. Alongside everything else we've discussed, positive affirmations can be a great way to combat that.

Using affirmations might sound a bit "new age" or nonsensical, but I'd be willing to bet money that any successful person you have *ever* heard of used them to create success. And hey, if it's good enough for Dale Carnegie, it's good enough for us, right?

The funny thing is, you're already using affirmations. Everyone does, they just don't always realize it. All that self-talk that you do, those things you say to yourself, those are your own, internal affirmations. Whenever you say to yourself things like:

- "What if something happens to me?"
- "I'll embarrass myself in public."
- "My heartbeat's racing, I'm going to die."
- "Something's wrong."
- "I'm not a happy person."

Those are examples of affirmations, and not good ones at that! But don't worry; it's not your fault. Even people that don't have anxiety often have very negative self-talk. Most people aren't aware of their own self-talk, yet it has such a powerful effect on their lives.

Effectively, the results we get are based on what we think. You get more of the tings that capture your focus. If you focus on the bad stuff, you're going to find more bad stuff. But if you *choose* to focus on the good stuff, you're going to see more of that!

How to use affirmations to beat anxiety

So we've established that you already have affirmations that you're using. You're just probably using them unconsciously. What we're going to do is *replace* those negative affirmations with positive ones.

The whole idea of affirmations is that they need to be repeated to yourself, consistently, in much the same way you unconsciously do already. Now you're choosing to repeat positive affirmations instead.

Your affirmations should be positive and reflective, generally describing the way you want to feel. For example:

- "My anxiety does not control me."
- "I am safe and protected."
- "I feel calm and at peace."
- "I have a great life and will continue to have a great life."
- "I know that I will be able to stop my panic attacks."

You can use these when you're anxious, but daily repetition is the most effective way to use them. Find ones you like from online, from friends, or write your own. Read through them aloud every morning. You can have as many or as few as you like, whatever works for you.

Overcome the "I don't believe in this nonsense" attitude

If you've not had any prior experience of using affirmations, they can seem a bit silly at first. Saying things that aren't true that you aren't sure are believable in the hopes it'll help you deal with anxiety is a bit of a stretch. The goal of affirmations is not to miraculously believe them or to cure your stress and anxiety instantly. The real purpose of affirmations is to take power away from the negative voice in your head. All the time spent repeating your positive affirmations is time the negative thoughts can't disrupt you.

Affirmations are something that can have profound effects while taking little time. They do have a few other benefits as well:

- **Creating A Positive Distraction.** Anxiety is something that can spiral and get worse when your thoughts run wild. Because of this, your coping tools should be something positive and uplifting. Using affirmations gives you that opportunity to repeat these types of uplifting phrases to yourself. This will distract your mind from your anxiety for a while and will also help you to focus on an uplifting idea.

- **Repetition Leads To Belief.** Your brain is constantly adapting to new stimulus. If it doesn't understand something, it changes to accommodate it. When you continually repeat a positive phrase to yourself that runs counter to the negative thoughts you usually think, it causes your brain to adapt to the new belief that you're repeating. This practice is based on the theory of Cognitive Dissonance, a very common phenomenon we see portrayed often with things like actors playing a part. Actors sometimes start to *"feel"* the same way as their character. Thankfully, you can use this to your advantage by getting the same benefits through affirmations.

- **Reinforcement of Positivity.** A big benefit of affirmations is to serve as a continual reminder to you to be and feel positive. They can be a great reminder of how you want to feel and what you're working towards.

Affirmations are rooted in the ideas of Neuro-Linguistic Programming, or NLP. In this context, it's the belief that positive affirmations repeated consistently can change a person's brain chemistry in a way that will promotes healing and positivity. NLP has its doubters amongst the science community, but it has a staunch following across the globe. I personally have had some very positive experiences with it and, if it doesn't work, at least there's no side effects!

How to maximize The benefits of affirmations

Your own affirmations should be expressions that have a meaning to you. If you search online, you'll be able to find hundreds of examples and these can be great to get you started. Ideally though, an affirmation should be something written in your own words and something that is entirely personal to you. This way, it'll mean more to you when you read it and it'll have a bigger impact.

For affirmations to be effective, you'll also need to read them on an ongoing basis. Given the way they work, you're not going to see a huge benefit from affirmations right way. You're probably going to feel a bit silly and awkward when you first start reading these things to yourself, but stick with it!

Affirmations will grow more and more effective the longer you use them. Your discomfort will lessen when reading them, making them feel more natural and, thus, more effective.

Again, remember that affirmations aren't a stand-alone

treatment for anxiety, but they can form a solid part of your own self-treatment.

So, what do I say?

Now you understand the benefits of affirmations, it's time to give you some examples to get started!

Feel free to use the list below or search online for some examples you feel might be a good fit to get you started. You don't have to use all of them; you simply need to pick and choose which ones work for you. There is no minimum for the number of affirmations you need; just go with whatever feels comfortable to you.

Example affirmations:

- I am cool, calm and collected.
- Every breath I breathe calms me, and every breath I release sends away tension.
- Every cell in my body is relaxed and calm.
- I love myself deeply and unconditionally.
- I am confident that I will solve life's problems successfully.
- I live in peace. I transcend stress of any kind.
- I am social and I enjoy meeting people.
- All is well in my world and I am safe.
- With every breath, I become more and more calm.
- With every breath, I release the anxiety within me.
- The future is positive. I look forward it with hope and happiness in my heart.

- I consistently overcome my fears and live my life courageously.
- I understand that the only constant in life, is change and am always prepared for it.
- I am free of anxiety and live my life to it's fullest.

When to use affirmations

As we've discussed, affirmations should be repeated daily for them to become effective. In the mornings is usually easiest. The simplest way is to read through them before or after brushing your teeth. That way, you'll be reminded to do it every morning and soon, they'll form part of your morning routine so you won't have think about doing them — you just will.

The only other main thing to note is that affirmations should be read aloud. Given this, most people want to do them when they're alone so they don't feel like crazy people talking to themselves! Another reason doing them around the same time you do your teeth is great because you're in a separate room, by yourself so you can feel more confident when reading them.

9

NEXT STEPS

hew! That was a lot of information. I hope you found the chapters and tools that were most relevant to you and got value from this book.

If you're still feeling a bit overwhelmed by all this information, don't worry! It really is simple. Just follow these steps and you'll be well on your way to beating anxiety.

ACTION PLAN

1. Learn to use the 4-7-8 breath to help to take control anxiety.
2. Try taking a natural supplement such as Rhodiola Rosea or L-Theanine.
3. Cut out caffeine (don't forget the *"Easy Plan to Quit Caffeine"* plan).
4. Get moving through exercise you can do daily.
5. Write positive affirmations and read them daily.

That's it. Simple steps to get you at least most of the way there and greatly reduce your ongoing anxiety. You can potentially stop your panic attacks and feel happier about your life!

Ultimately, there's always something you can do to make your life better. This book is teaching you how to regain control of your life. Then it's up to you what you do with your freedom!

BOOK 2:

Beating Panic Attacks - *5 Simple Steps To Eliminate Panic Attacks Effortlessly*

INTRODUCTION

I want to thank you and congratulate you for downloading the book, *Beating Panic Attacks: 5 simple steps to eliminate panic attacks effortlessly.*

This book contains proven steps and strategies on how to completely eliminate panic attacks in 5 simple steps to regain control of your life quickly and easily.

This book also contains a brief overview of panic attacks and panic disorders. It tells you their definitions as well as their common causes and symptoms. Learning about panic attacks and panic disorders can really help you to prepare yourself in case you experience a familiar symptom.

Moreover, this book discusses the five easy techniques and strategies to use if you want to overcome your panic attack quickly and effectively. These steps are about using breathing techniques and meditation to improve your condition so you can regain control of your life.

Thanks again for downloading this book, I hope you enjoy it!

10

WHAT ARE PANIC ATTACKS?

*P*anic attacks are shitty. Let me just put that out there. If you've ever experienced one, you know what I'm talking about.

The annoying thing is, it's your body just doing its job. It thinks that you're in danger so it kicks in your fight or flight response.

Google defines a panic attack as:

"a sudden feeling of acute and disabling anxiety."

Which seems to sum it up nicely...bummer.

Some people experience panic attacks rarely and others have an on-going struggle with them, sometimes on a daily basis. If that's you, I feel your pain, I feel your struggle and just know, there are many, really simple fixes for it that you can start to implement *today*.

Personally, when I was suffering with these attacks, I had

extreme agoraphobia and could barely leave my room. Later on, I had massive anxiety around driving, especially on motorways and would feel an attack coming on if I just thought about having to drive on one.

There's not always a rhyme or reason for why panic attacks happen. Sometimes, like with me and my driving on motorways, it was pretty obvious what would set it off. I had extreme anxiety around a specific situation.

I also had panic attacks out of the blue with no reason whatsoever, in situations I had been in many times before without issue.

I had one at dinner with my better half's family once…that was fun.

According to statistics, at least one in every ten individuals experiences a panic attack at some point. Likewise, at least one in every fifty individuals suffers from panic disorder.

In the US alone, over 60 million people experience panic attacks and over 3 million people suffer from panic disorder —this is how common panic attacks and panic disorder are! So don't worry, you're not alone!

The Signs and Symptoms of Panic Attack

The signs and symptoms of panic attacks tend to show abruptly. They usually reach the peak within a few minutes and may last up to 30 minutes (usually a lot less!) and come sometimes come in waves.

People who experience a panic attack usually find that they experience one or more of the following:

- Dizziness
- Shortness of breath
- Sweating
- Stomachache
- Lightheadedness
- Hyperventilation
- Dry mouth
- Chest pain
- Numbness
- Shaking
- Tingling sensations
- Hot and cold flashes
- Choking feeling
- Fear of losing sanity
- Fear of dying

If you experience a panic attack and you notice any of it's physical symptoms, you may, incorrectly, think you have a physical disorder because of the very real symptoms you experience in the moment. This is not the case. Seriously. You've been through panic attacks before and you're fine right? No heart attacks, you're still sane, no ongoing health issues etc. Likewise, even if you feel that you're really about to die, there is a huge chance that you're actually not.

The symptoms of panic attacks occur prior to you having an overdrive of nervous impulses coming from your brain towards the other parts of your body. So when you have a panic attack, your body may release more hormones, including adrenaline. This prompts you to have a *fight or flight* response.

The fight or flight response is something that is ingrained in your system. It started with our ancestors from the Paleolithic era when they either had to fight the danger in front of them or flee to stay safe and alive. At present, we still experience the fight or flight response whenever we are faced with a dangerous situation, or at least, a situation we perceive as dangerous.

What you might find is that your body may have the same reaction when you experience a panic attack. You may hyperventilate or breathe very heavily. As you do this, you breathe out large amounts of carbon dioxide, causing the acidity of your blood to change. This leads to more symptoms such as cramps, confusion, and sometimes fainting (very rare!).

This imbalance isn't really harmful at all as, once you calm down, the body will naturally balance everything out again. It's basically just a case of breathing slower.

If you recognize yourself in anything you just read, don't worry! There are some fantastic tools and techniques to overcome this and regain control of your life today!

The Causes of Panic Attacks

Experts have not been able to pinpoint any exact cause of panic attack, but they have found that genetics and family history have something to do with it. Those whose family members have panic disorder are also more likely to have it.

In addition, panic attacks can be triggered by exposure to stressful situations like speaking in public or crossing a bridge and even some food and drinks can have an impact as we'll discuss later.

Overcoming Panic Attacks & Panic Disorders

Now, all of that sounds a bit doom and gloom, but fear not! There are some amazing tools and techniques to overcome these issues. Many of which you will find, have an immediate impact, and the others will help you to be more relaxed and happier on an on-going basis.

Let's get to it shall we!

BODY & MIND

STEP 1 – PRACTICE MINDFULNESS
MEDITATION

*M*indfulness or mindfulness meditation is one of the most effective and highly recommended natural treatments for panic disorders. This technique is all about being aware of your present moment without making any judgments.

Through this technique, you can learn how to see things more clearly as well as being able to become more focused on your present situation. According to a study conducted by researchers at Lund University in Sweden, mindfulness is just as effective as cognitive behavioral therapy, which is all about replacing negative thinking patterns with positive ones.

In another study conducted at Boston University, researchers have found that mindfulness helps people with depression and anxiety let go of negative thoughts and stop obsessing over them. At the end of the study, the participants were able to get out of their depressive or anxious loop.

Furthermore, researchers have found that mindfulness meditation can help you sleep better, regulate mood levels, and alleviate stress, allowing you to relax and prevent panic attacks from occurring.

If you want your quality of life to improve, there is no doubt that mindfulness meditation can really be helpful and the beautiful part is;

It's so wonderfully easy to learn!

Why Mindfulness Meditation?

Mindfulness mediation sounds a bit airy-fairy. Yes. Of course it does. It conjures images of hippies or monks sitting on top of a mountain gently murmuring *"oooommmmm"* to themselves. Whilst that's not exactly the type of mediation we're talking about here, they seem like pretty chilled out guys right? Maybe they're on to something with the whole *meditation* thing.

What we're talking about is an incredible tool to tap into the present moment. Ultimately, what this helps you to do is see the symptoms you're having and view them *objectively*.

Why is this so important? Well, if you've ever experienced a panic attack, you can probably attest to the fact that, regardless of what starts it, when you're in the middle of it, you're only ever thinking about the worst situation and being about as far from objective as you can be.

"I'm having a heart attack, I'm going to die. OMG my family are going to be sad. What have I done with my life?" and so on.

What the practice of being mindful brings you is the ability to take a step back from the moment, look at the symptoms objectively and say;

"Ahhh, I see there's a bit of a tight chest feeling. That's OK. It doesn't mean I'm having a heart attack. It is what it is."

"I see that there are all these thoughts about how I feel I might be going insane. That's OK. I don't need to understand these thoughts, I just need to notice them for what they are."

"Looking at all these symptoms I can see that really, this is my body's reaction to something. My body is over-reacting because it thinks I am in danger. But I'm not. I will observe these symptoms until they pass and go about my day."

How to Practice Mindfulness Meditation

The short answer is:

Take a seat, pay attention to your breath, and when you notice your attention has wandered, return your attention to the breath.

For a slightly more in-depth run through:

- Find good posture with your back upright and relaxed in a chair or on a cushion. You can use a blanket and a pillow, although a good cushion that will last you a lifetime of practice. You can sit in a chair with your feet on the floor, loosely cross-legged, in lotus posture (if you're that flexible), kneeling etc. However you sit is fine, as long as you're comfortable. Just make sure you are stable and upright. If the constraints of your body prevent you from sitting erect, just find a comfortable position you can stay in for a while.

- Once you're sitting comfortably, start to feel your breath as it goes in and out. Really try to follow the breath all the way through your mouth, into your lungs, filling your belly, and then back out again.
- Inevitably, your attention will leave the breath and wander to other places. This happens to everyone. It's literally part of the practice so don't stress about doing it wrong!
- When you do notice this, weather that's in a few seconds, a minute or five minutes, just return your attention to the breath. Don't worry about judging yourself or obsessing over the content of the thoughts.
- You focus. Your mind wanders. You notice this and re-focus on the breath, and repeat. That's the practice.

It's incredibly simple, but it's not necessarily easy. Just keep doing it and you'll get the results.

It's not as easy as saying *"I command myself to quit thinking of anything else besides my breath that I have decided to focus on."* Because you'll find yourself thinking about cat food or whatever. The point is that you *realize* you have strayed off course.

Then you can gently bring your attention back to the breath and become present again.

Practice letting go of things you don't have control over. Oftentimes, people become anxious and experience panic attacks simply because they keep worrying about certain things happening or not happening.

For example; you can't control accidents, natural calamities, feelings of other people, and a whole host of other things. Remember that you're not a God (unless you are, in which case, nice to meet you Mr. God), you're a human being. You can't control everything, no matter how much you want to.

So when you get into an accident or when a loved one passes away, there is nothing else to do but to accept the fact and move on. Always try to see the positive side of the incident, however hard it might be at the time.

Say, you are currently going through a divorce. Instead of viewing it as a huge loss, you can view it as a chance for a new beginning.

When you start looking for and focusing on the positives of everything, you'll find more of them. If you naturally have more good and positive things in your life, doesn't it stand to reason that you'll be happier with less anxiety?

In addition, your blood pressure will normalize. Oftentimes, stress and anxiety causes blood pressure to rise. In order to bring it back to its normal level, you need to let your blood vessels dilate. You can help this by taking a few deep breaths and releasing tension.

Interestingly, anxiety does not only affect your mind, but it also affects your body. It can actually trigger numerous physical changes and symptoms. Excessive anxiety can trigger the fight or flight response of your system, causing your lymphatic nervous system to release the stress hormone cortisol. This, in turn, can raise your blood sugar levels and triglycerides.

It can also cause shortness of breath, dizziness, dry mouth, nausea, sweating, and panic attacks.

The real positive of this is, once you get your anxiety in check with these steps, you may find some potentially long-standing health issues are alleviated, or at least lessened. When you practice relaxation techniques you trigger your relaxation response, which is characterized by warm feelings and a silent mental alertness.

Cool, huh?

STEP 2 – PRACTICE BODY SCANNING

*B*ody scan meditation is a popular practice for alleviating stress. If you have a panic disorder or suffer from any sort of anxiety, practicing this technique can really help you prevent panic attacks and alleviate any background worries. It is actually very similar to progressive muscle relaxation, except that it involves focusing on the sensations of your body parts rather than relaxing and tensing the muscles.

How to Practice Body Scan Meditation

Body Scan Meditation is kind of similar to the mindfulness meditation we just discussed in it's practice and application. You're doing something that brings you into the present moment.

Here's a great, in-depth run through of the steps for the awesome, StillMind:

1. Sit in a chair as for the breath awareness or lie down, making yourself comfortable, lying on your back on a mat or rug on the floor or on your bed. Choose a place where you will be warm and undisturbed. Allow your eyes to close gently.

2. Take a few moments to get in touch with the movement of your breath and the sensations in the body when you are ready, bring your awareness to the physical sensations in your body, especially to the sensations of touch or pressure, where your body makes contact with the chair or bed. On each outbreath, allow yourself to let go, to sink a little deeper into the chair or bed.

3. Remind yourself of the intention of this practice. Its aim is not to feel any different, relaxed, or calm; this may happen or it may not. Instead, the intention of the practice is, as best you can, to bring awareness to any sensations you detect, as you focus your attention on each part of the body in turn.

4. Now bring your awareness to the physical sensations in the lower abdomen, becoming aware of the changing patterns of sensations in the abdominal wall as you breathe in, and as you breathe out. Take a few minutes to feel the sensations as you breathe in and as you breathe out.

5. Having connected with the sensations in the abdomen, bring the focus or "spotlight" of your awareness down the left leg, into the left foot, and out to the toes of the left foot. Focus on each of the toes of the left foot in turn, bringing a gentle curiosity to investigate the quality of the sensations you find, perhaps noticing the sense of contact between the toes, a sense of tingling, warmth, or no particular sensation.

6. When you are ready, on an inbreath, feel or imagine the breath entering the lungs, and then passing down into the abdomen, into the left leg, the left foot, and out to the toes of the left foot. Then, on the outbreath, feel or imagine the breath coming all the way back up, out of the foot, into the leg, up through the abdomen, chest, and out through the nose. As best you can, continue this for a few breaths, breathing down into the toes, and back out from the toes. It may be difficult to get the hang of this just practice this "breathing into" as best you can, approaching it playfully.

7. Now, when you are ready, on an outbreath, let go of awareness of the toes, and bring your awareness to the sensations on the bottom of your left foot—bringing a gentle, investigative awareness to the sole of the foot, the instep, the heel (e.g., noticing the sensations where the heel makes contact with the mat or bed). Experiment with "breathing with" the sensations—being aware of the breath in the background, as, in the foreground, you explore the sensations of the lower foot.

8. Now allow the awareness to expand into the rest of the foot—to the ankle, the top of the foot, and right into the bones and joints. Then, taking a slightly deeper breath, directing it down into the whole of the left foot, and, as the breath lets go on the outbreath, let go of the left foot completely, allowing the focus of awareness to move into the lower left leg—the calf, shin, knee, and so on, in turn.

9. Continue to bring awareness, and a gentle curiosity, to the physical sensations in each part of the rest of the body in turn - to the upper left leg, the right toes, right foot, right leg, pelvic area, back, abdomen, chest, fingers, hands, arms, shoulders, neck, head, and face. In each area, as best you can, bring the same detailed level of awareness and gentle curiosity to the bodily sensations present. As you leave each major area, "breathe in" to it on the inbreath, and let go of that region on the outbreath.

10. When you become aware of tension, or of other intense sensations in a particular part of the body, you can "breathe in" to them —using the inbreath gently to bring awareness right into the sensations, and, as best you can, have a sense of their letting go, or releasing, on the outbreath.

11. The mind will inevitably wander away from the breath and the body from time to time. That is entirely normal. It is what minds do. When you notice it, gently acknowledge it, noticing where the mind has gone off to, and then gently return your attention to the part of the body you intended to focus on.

After you have "scanned" the whole body in this way, spend a few minutes being aware of a sense of the body as a whole, and of the breath flowing freely in and out of the body.

If you find yourself falling asleep, you might find it helpful to prop your head up with a pillow, open your eyes, or do the practice sitting up rather than lying down.

You can adjust the time spent in this practice by using larger chunks of your body to become aware of or spending a shorter or longer time with each part.

STEP 3 – PRACTICE ANCHORING

*I*t is not always easy to control your nerves. You need sufficient skills. Just think of it this way; You've been asked to give a speech. This is something that you have always dreamt of doing. You know that if you do well, you'll probably get a raise, you'll be able to buy that nice house you've always wanted... However, you've got those telltale butterflies in your stomach.

So what can you do about this? What if there was a magic button you could press that would give you instant calm and confidence? Well guess what...

What is Anchoring?

In NLP (neuro linguistic programming), anchoring refers to the process of associating an emotional response with a trigger so that the response may be quickly and powerfully changed.

In our case, this means you can use anchoring to associate a calm mental state with a simple internal trigger to help calm down and eliminate anxiety quickly.

You do this by anchoring states of mind so you can fire the anchor and establish the state instantly.

A brief history:

Anchoring is kind of like Pavlov's experiments with dogs. Pavlov sounded a bell as the animal was given food. The animals salivated when they saw the food. After doing this a few times, the bell and the food being shown together, the bell alone made the dogs salivate. Poor dogs.

Anchors are stimuli that call forth states of mind - thoughts and emotions. For example, touching a knuckle of the left hand could be an anchor. Some anchors are involuntary. So the smell of bread may take you back to your childhood. A tune may remind you of a loved one. A touch can bring back memories and the past states. These anchors work automatically and you may not be aware of the triggers.

Establishing an anchor means producing the stimuli (the anchor) when the desired state is experienced so that the desired state is pared to the anchor.

Anchors can be visual, auditory or kinesthetic and can be quick and easy install (just like a piece of software.)

Installing Anchors

It's quite a simple process and once it's done, you can use the anchor whenever you need that little boost of calmness.

1. Decide on the state you want to anchor. For example being calm and relaxed.

2. Choose an anchor (or anchors) that you wish to trigger the desired state.

3. Recall a memory or imagine a situation where you can experience the state. So recall or imagine a time when you experienced being really calm and relaxed. A lazy afternoon on a beach or a chilled evening with your friends watching TV for example.

4. Active the anchor or anchors when the experience is vivid and you are in the desired state.

5. Release the anchors when the experience begins to fade. If you keep applying the anchor when the experience is fading, then you will anchor a drop in calmness and relaxation!

6. Do something else - open your eyes ... count down from 10 to break state and distract yourself.

7. Repeat the steps several times, each time making the memory more vivid. This is not actually required when the anchor is established at the high point of the experience. However, you can strengthen the anchor by establishing it at the high point of several such experiences.

8. Apply the anchor and check that the required state occurs.

9. Future pace the situation where you want to experience the desired state. Fire the anchor to check that it creates a sufficiently resourced state.

10. Check the anchor the next day to ensure it is a permanent anchor.

Tips for anchoring

- The anchor (or anchors) should be fired in exactly the same way every time you link them to the resourceful experience.
- Anchor at the high point of the experience containing the resourceful state.
- If you do not experience the state when future pacing and especially if you experience anxiety, then stop applying the anchor. (You will anchor the negative state!)
- There is a knowingness which makes anchoring work that is established by the unconscious mind.
- You can strengthen the anchor by repeating the above process over several days.
- If you are in a situation where you experience the desired state in reality, then you can reestablish the anchor to that situation.

Anchoring can be an incredibly powerful tool to help overcome anxiety in the moment. It's also really useful for any other state you could want to have on demand.

Want to feel more energized? *Make an anchor.*

Want to feel more in love? *Make an anchor.*

There's almost endless possibilities, but for the purposes of this book, just make one that makes you feel calm. If you have a panic attack and you've for a calm anchor set, it will bring you back to calmness in an instant and that's really what we want isn't it?

BREATHING

14

STEP 4 – PRACTICE SIMPLE
BREATHING TECHNIQUES

*B*reathing techniques are highly effective in stress management and panic attack prevention. You can practice them whenever and wherever you are. So even if you can't get away from a stressful situation, you can still calm yourself down and prevent the onset of a panic attack.

These techniques let you experience relief from stress without going anywhere. You can stay at your desk and perform breathing exercises. You can do them while you're driving. You can do them while you're out with friends and in this way, you will always have a tool to use whenever you feel anxious and you can quickly and easily calm yourself.

Now you can try a million and one breathing exercises (and I suggest that you do). You can spend hours on YouTube and on blogs trying the different methods, but for me, one technique stands out above all the rest. It's so simple, so quick and so effective. I use it to calm me down if I'm having a panic attack or a feel one coming on. I use it to fall asleep. I use it to relax if I'm nervous about making a speech. I use it for anything and everything.

The 4 – 7 – 8 Exercise

If you only take away 1 thing from this book, **let it be this**.

This little technique has had the *biggest impact* for me in reducing my panic attacks.

"The 4-7-8 Breathing Exercise" also called *"The Relaxing Breath"* is based on pranayama, an ancient Indian practice that means *"regulation of breath."* The exercise is described by Dr. Andrew Weil as *"a natural tranquilizer for the nervous system"* that eases the body into a state of calmness and relaxation. Sounds good right?

There are different theories as to why it works so well but mainly the belief is that it encourages the fast removal of carbon dioxide from the body.

Dr. Weil's technique is beautifully simple, takes pretty much no time, and can be done anywhere in just five steps. Although you can do the exercise in any position, it's recommended to sit with your back straight while learning the exercise, kind of like the position we discussed for meditation.

Dr. Weil explains to "place the tip of your tongue against the ridge of tissue just behind your upper front teeth and keep it there through the entire exercise. You will be exhaling through your mouth around your tongue; try pursing your lips slightly if this seems awkward." This is followed by the five-step procedure listed below:

1. Exhale completely through your mouth, making a whoosh sound.
2. Close your mouth and inhale quietly through your nose to a mental count of four.
3. Hold your breath for a count of seven.
4. Exhale completely through your mouth, making a whoosh sound to a count of eight.
5. This is one breath. Now inhale again and repeat the cycle three more times for a total of four breaths.

Dr. Weil emphasizes the most important part of this process is holding your breath for eight seconds. This is because keeping the breath in will allow oxygen to fill your lungs and then circulate throughout the body. It is this that produces a relaxing effect in the body.

I've said it before and I'll say it again:

THIS ONE TECHNEQUE WILL RID YOU OF A PANIC ATTACK

If you feel one coming on or you're in the middle of one, just run through a couple of cycles of this breathing exercise and you'll be calm in no time!

15

STEP 5 – PRACTICE YOGIC BREATHING

*S*ometimes when your day becomes too stressful to handle, you may have a hard time sleeping at night. Some people have bedtime rituals, like; lighting a scented candle, writing in a journal, meditating, or drinking chamomile tea (I'm more of an English Breakfast tea kind of guy, but whatever floats your boat).

If meditation is not exactly your thing, you can still reap similar benefits without practicing it. Yoga incorporates a couple of breathing techniques that you may find to be useful.

Don't worry. I'm not going to ask you to fold yourself into any crazy yoga positions. I can't do any of that myself. What is laid out below is further breathing exercises that have been used for literally hundreds of years by the yogic community with some pretty solid results.

Alternate Nostril Breathing

This yogic breathing technique promotes deep relaxation through the balance of the right and left sides of the brain as the nervous system is calmed down.

- **Sit down with both of your legs crossed or propped up on a pillow.** You can also kneel down next to the bed. Feel free to use blankets or any other object that can provide you with adequate support.
- **Rest your left hand over your left thigh.** The fingers on your right hand should be extended as if you are trying to wave at someone. Bend your middle and index fingers so that they curl inside your palm.
- **Put your thumb on the side of your nose and slightly touch your nostrils.** When you touch your nostrils, be careful not to be constricting. The idea is to limit airflow temporarily to one nostril.
- **Take a deep inhale and then exhale.** Close off your right nostril using your thumb. Breathe in through your left nostril for four seconds. When you reach the peak of that breath, you should close off your left nostril using your ring finger.
- **For four counts, hold this position to retain the breath.** Release your right nostril and breathe out for four seconds.
- **Then, take a deep breath for four seconds through your right nostril.** Just like what you did before, close it off, hold the position, and retain your breath for four seconds. Release your left nostril as you breathe out fully for four seconds. Take a deep breath through your left nostril and repeat the entire cycle.

You can do this breathing technique as often as you want. When you're done, you can have a lie down on your bed and doze off or continue on with your day in a more relaxed state.

Deep Throat Breathing

This yoga breathing technique relaxes the body and calms the mind. You'll need to be in bed or on a comfortable floor for this one.

- **Simply lie down on your back with your legs wide apart.** Keep them as wide as your hips. Relax your arms at your sides and close your eyes.
- **Breathe in deeply through your nose and breathe out through your mouth.** With every breath you take, you should fill your lungs totally. Similarly, with every exhale you do, breathe out completely.
- **After taking three deep breaths,** inhale through your nose for four counts while constricting the back of your throat a bit. This way, you will feel as if you are breathing through a straw at the back of your throat as well as filling your lungs with air.
- **You should notice the sound of your breath mimicking the sound of waves that come in and out.** This sound is actually very helpful in making you fall asleep. You can compare it to the soft snore of a baby.
- **Hold your breath at the top for four seconds as you silently observe your feelings.** You should aim to

feel relaxed and full. Breathe out through your nose for four seconds while constricting your throat a little.

- Once your lungs have released all the air, you should begin to fill them again.
- Take a deep breath for six seconds and hold it for another six seconds.
- Finally, breathe out for six seconds.
- Repeat this breathing process, adding two seconds more for every cycle.

After you reached your maximum capacity of breathing and holding, you can begin taking away a couple of seconds at a time. So, if twelve seconds is the maximum amount of time that you can do, your next round should be down to ten seconds. Continue subtracting two seconds every time, so the next round is eight seconds, and so on.

When you reach four seconds, you can release everything and return to normal breathing. Now that you have relaxed your mind and body, you can have a peaceful sleep and wake up feeling refreshed and rejuvenated.

DIET

16

WHAT YOU EAT EFFECTS YOUR BRAIN

"YOU ARE WHAT YOU EAT."

e've all heard it. It's usually a well-meant comment from someone trying to steer you away from chips and a burger toward something a bit more green and healthy.

I used to dismiss this, especially in my younger years. I thought I could eat what I wanted (usually a big bowl of pasta) and be fine. And that *was* the case...for a while.

At some point or another in my late teens, I lost my job. At the time this was the best thing that had ever happened to me.

"So you're saying I can go to bed when I want, sleep for 13 hours, get up when I want and basically spend my days doing nothing and chilling?...Sign me up, that sounds awesome!"

That was pretty much the attitude. A lot's changed since then and I am not the same person I was. I'm up early every day improving myself and working towards big goals, but at the time, this lazy mentality made sense to me.

The point is, at the time I got into a routine of sleeping a lot, waking up, eating a big bowl of pasta and cheese (similar to mac & cheese for our American friends, just without the lovely baked finish) and then feeling tired, zoned out and uninspired for the rest of the day.

I was sleeping for 12-13 hours a day and I was still tired all the time. What's that about?

Unsurprisingly, this *"life without any goals"* happened to be around the time anxiety & depression first visited me. Coincidence? I think not.

I found a stark change in my energy and anxiety came when I found a job and started eating "better" at work. My anxiety went. My depression went. I was happier _because_ I was healthier.

As you can probably guess by the title of the chapter, my opinion on the matter is pretty resolute:

WHAT YOU EAT AFFECTS YOUR MOOD!

There are so many studies on how gut bacteria affect your mood and there are so many studies on how different foods effect how you feel.

As a simple example;

Have you ever eaten lunch?...I thought so. Now, have you ever eaten a *BIG* lunch? I'm talking a couple of sandwiches, maybe some pasta, a fizzy drink and a chocolate or doughnut to finish it off?

Now tell me, how did you feel about an hour after that?

Did you feel like you were about to fall asleep and you couldn't think quite as clearly as before? Did you feel a bit slow and lethargic for the rest of the day? Most likely. If not, you're some sort of medical anomaly and you could make good money selling your body to science.

This is just a really simple illustration as to how food can immediately affect your mind and physiology.

It's not too much of a stretch then, if this extra bit of sugar at lunch can affect you so drastically, that eating a sub-optimal diet can contribute to other things over the long term, namely, anxiety and panic attacks.

We already know that excess carbohydrates cause obesity (don't worry, this isn't turning into a diet book). With the global rise in obesity, we're seeing a strong correlation with a rise in neuro-degenerative diseases such as Alzheimer's which a number of scientists have called to be re-labeled Type 3 diabetes as it results from resistance to insulin in the brain.

What science is saying then, is that excess carbohydrates, in vast quantities over a period of years, can cause serious damage in the body and mind.

BUT...

The good news is; there is *always* something you can do about it.

The answer seems to be eating a lower carbohydrate and a higher, healthy fat diet.

Why you ask?

We're starting to see strong evidence for healthy fats improving cognitive function in patients with Alzheimer's.

If that sentence alone doesn't excite you, the same concept is being applied in other areas of medicine and there's a lot of scientists getting really excited about the fact that a low carb, high fat (ketogenic) diet seems to have some pretty profound effect on inflammation in the body and a whole heap of other stuff.

I tried going on a ketogenic diet for 30 days. And I had…0 panic attacks. I started eating carbs again and they started to come back.

I've also experimented with eliminating caffeine (well, coffee anyway, I'm British so there's no way I'm not going to drink tea) and have had some pretty profound results with it.

No more caffeine = No more anxiety*

*For me at least!

Now I don't want this chapter to be a pitch for a low-carb lifestyle, you'll find endless books and blogs proclaiming it to be the best thing since sliced bread (pun intended). What I wanted to show you was that what you eat can really effect how you feel and preform.

So when I say; *Try giving up caffeine for 30 days and watch your anxiety lessen...*

I know it works, and this chapter is about showing you that.

What you put into your body makes a big difference on your anxiety and panic response also.

So, eat better and feel better because of it!

NEXT STEPS

17

QUICK START GUIDE

*S*o this is all well and good. But how do you actually implement any of this?

Well, let's keep it simple;

1. Try the 4/7/8 breathing method whenever you feel a panic attack coming on and any other time you want to just relax…Try it now…go on, I'll wait.
2. Cut out caffeine (just for 30 days) – You can get back to your double, triple mocha late crap after a month if you feel it hasn't made a difference
3. Start practicing mindfulness meditation daily – It only needs to take 10 minutes. If you only had to spend 10 minutes a day on something and it eliminated your anxiety and panic attacks, would you do it? Exactly, that's what I thought.

The idea with any of the techniques in the book is to practice them at a time when you don't need them, so you can easily call upon them when you do need them.

Most of these can be performed anywhere, any time and without anyone really noticing. Even if you have to excuse yourself for a minute or two and run through a couple of deep breathing cycles in the restroom, it's not quite as much of an inconvenience as having a panic attack whilst at your desk at work!

So get practicing and you'll find your anxiety begins to lessen and lessen further until you can really live your life to the fullest!

You always have choices and choosing to eliminate anxiety seems like a pretty sound one.

AFTERWORD

Panic attacks can be a horrible experience for anyone but, given the right tools and techniques, anyone can overcome them and live a full life.

The methods outlined in this book will help you to take charge again so, if you ever feel another attack coming on, you have everything you need to regain control again, quickly.

You've now got the tools to work towards lessening the frequency of the attacks until they're just a distant memory.

You can do it. It's not even that difficult. If you truly want to change and rid yourself of panic attacks, the steps outlined in this book will get you there.

Now go out there and live your life on your terms!!!

THANK YOU

Thank you again for downloading this book!

I hope this book was able to help you to eliminate panic attacks and regain control of your life.

The next step is to go out there and live your life to the fullest!

Finally, if you enjoyed this book, then I'd like to ask you for a favor, would you be kind enough to leave a review for this book on Amazon? It'd be greatly appreciated!

Thank you and good luck!

Ed Jones

ABOUT THE AUTHOR

I'm Edward Jones. I was a normal guy, living a normal life. Then, over the course of a few months, my mental health started to deteriorate while anxiety, panic attacks and depression took over my life.

These problems steadily got worse and worse. Nothing was helping. I spoke to my doctor (who wanted to put me on drugs), but I made the decision I wasn't going to go down that route. At my worst point, I could barely leave my room without having massive anxiety and panic attacks.

It was then I decided to fix myself, no matter what.

That decision lead me down the path of researching and trying some of the most effective ways to control and eliminate anxiety, panic attacks and depression. It was a slow road to recovery, but it's been worth every second of it. I have my life back now and I'm happier than I've ever been!

Once I figured out what worked and sorted myself out, I felt compelled to share my newfound knowledge and help as many others in the same situation as I could.

I plan to write a few books to get everything out there and I'd love to engage with anyone that's struggling with anxiety or depression. The most powerful thing can sometimes be knowing that someone has gone through what you're going through, and that there is a solution.

I've been there, I feel your pain and I would love to help you get your life back!

I'd love to hear from anyone who would like to talk more about these issues. You can reach me at ed@edjonesbooks.com or via my website; http://edjonesbooks.com/

FREE AUDIOBOOK

Thank you so much for taking the time to read this book. I truly hope you got value from it and, more than anything, I hope you were able to use the tools in here to overcome the challenges you're facing.

I understand that the steps in here are most useful if you can refer back to them periodically and sometimes audio is the best way to do this.

That's why I spent a good deal of time finding a narrator and getting a high-quality audiobook produced for you. You can find it on Audible and even get a FREE copy by signing up using the following link:

https://tinyurl.com/edjonesfreebook

Full disclosure, that is an affiliate link which helps to support me and my writing, but if you don't want to use that link, feel free to sign up separately...I won't be offended!